Hypertext in Context

The Cambridge Series on Electronic Publishing

Managing Editor: P. HAMMERSLEY

The purpose of this new series is to publish books in the exciting and topical field of electronic printing and publishing. The series will attempt to cover all aspects of electronic publishing including:

- Matters relating to hardware, software and standards concerned with transferring authors' words and images to the printed page;

- Screen-based documents — hypertext and its implications for authors and readers;

- Document delivery — electronic methods of reader access to publications, full-text database publishing, CD-ROM delivery systems and the impact for libraries;

- On-line publishing systems and distributed publication systems — the impact of networks on the publication process;

- Human factors relating, for example, to document structures for readability, editing aids, expert-system based interfaces, and type and page design.

While there will be some overlap with other areas of computer science (such as information retrieval, HCI and computer graphics), the series will concentrate primarily on books concerned with publishing, and so should provide a scholarly and specific survey of developments in this subject area.

Titles will range from advanced textbooks to multi-author works.

Already Published:

EP88, Document Manipulation and Typography; J.C. van Vliet (ed).
Structured Documents; J. André, R. Furuta & V. Quint (eds).
Raster Imaging and Digital Typography 89; J. André & R. Hersch (eds).
EP90, R. Furuta (ed)
Hypertext: concepts, systems & applications, N. Streitz, A. Rizk, & J. André (eds)

Hypertext in Context

Cliff McKnight,
Principal Scientist, HUSAT Research Institute, Loughborough University
Andrew Dillon,
Senior Project Officer, HUSAT Research Institute, Loughborough University
John Richardson,
Senior Project Officer, HUSAT Research Institute, Loughborough University

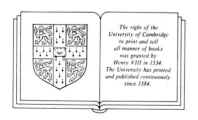

The right of the
University of Cambridge
to print and sell
all manner of books
was granted by
Henry VIII in 1534.
The University has printed
and published continuously
since 1584.

CAMBRIDGE UNIVERSITY PRESS

Cambridge

New York   Port Chester   Melbourne   Sydney

Published by the Press Syndicate of the University of Cambridge
The Pitt Building, Trumpington Street, Cambridge CB2 1RP
40 West 20th Street, New York, NY 10011-4211, USA
10 Stamford Road, Oakleigh, Melbourne 3166, Australia

First published 1991

Printed in Great Britain at the University Press, Cambridge

Library of Congress cataloguing in publication data available

British Library cataloguing in publication data available

ISBN 0 521 37488 X

CONTENTS

ACKNOWLEDGEMENTS

We are grateful to the British Library Research and Development Department for funding much of the research through which our ideas have developed. We are also grateful to the Research Committee of Loughborough University for funding some of the time necessary to write this book.

We gratefully acknowledge Taylor & Francis Ltd for permission to make the electronic copies of the journal *Behaviour and Information Technology* as described in Chapter 7.

We are also extremely grateful to Denise McKnight, Hilary Dyer and Arthur Gardner for constructive comments on various sections of the book, although what remains is our fault, not theirs!

Bibliographic records require a serial list of authors. In a hypertext world it need not be so...

CHAPTER ONE

HOW DID WE GET HERE?

> *"Intertwingularity is not generally acknowledged — people keep pretending they can make things hierarchical, categorizable and sequential when they can't. Everything is deeply intertwingled."*
>
> Ted Nelson: Dream Machines

Introduction

The origins of hypertext can be traced back through some considerable length of time — for example, in his often-cited introductory article, Conklin (1987) makes passing reference to the Talmud and the work of Aristotle, and in the past there was certainly an appreciation of the inter-connectedness of information. If this is the case, why has hypertext suddenly become the focus of so much attention?

In fact, like most 'overnight' successes, hypertext hasn't *suddenly* arrived. Several research groups in academic institutions and industrial concerns have been developing and using hypertext systems since the 1960s. What *has* developed rapidly in recent years is the ready availability of an enabling technology — the computer. While it is certainly true that the ideas underlying hypertext have been around for many years, it is the vastly increased availability of computing power that has allowed the implementation, elaboration and exploration of these ideas.

As recently as 1964, the computing effort of the entire British academic community was handled by a single Ferranti Atlas machine housed in the Science and Engineering Research Council's Rutherford Appleton Laboratory. These days, all academics have ready access to mainframe computers and many also make extensive use of minicomputers and personal microcomputers. Hypertext has made the same journey, from mainframe to micro, and in the process has gone from academic research area to commercial software venture. Hypertext packages are now potentially 'big business' and consequently forces other than research results or practical experience are being exerted on the field.

In this book we will explore the tripartite themes of *people* using computer-based *information* to perform a *task* in what has come to be known as a hypertext (or, more generally, hypermedia[1]) environment. At times we may focus on one aspect at the expense of the other two, but it should be remembered that a proper consideration of hypertext necessarily involves all three.

It is perhaps a fitting irony that the best way to disseminate our views is via the paper-based medium of a book. In 1982, Jonassen predicted that "in ten years or so the book as we know it will be as obsolete as is movable type today" (Jonassen, 1982, p.379) — a sentiment which apparently echoed the feeling of the pioneer Ted Nelson 20 years earlier, although in a lecture delivered in 1989 Nelson said he had thought books would be a thing of the past within five years, that is, by 1967 (Nelson, 1989). From our point of view, books will be a feature of information dissemination for many years to come. In this book, therefore, the relevant question will not be "when will hypertext replace books?" but rather "when is it better to present the information via hypertext rather than via paper?" When we talk about hypertext, we are talking about *people* using *information* to perform a *task*. and hence we will be concerned to elucidate the nature of the tasks which are best supported by the medium.

What is hypertext?

What, then, are the ideas which have become the centre of a vast research effort and the subject of several large academic conferences in recent years? Simply stated, hypertext consists of *nodes* (or 'chunks') of information and *links* between them. Stated thus, it is easy to find early examples of hypertext — any text which references another can be seen as two nodes of information with the reference forming the link; any text which uses footnotes can be seen as containing nodes of information (the text and the footnote), with the footnote marker providing the link or pointer from one node to the other. As we shall see later, the idea of a node is very general, and there are no 'rules' about how big a node should be or what it should contain. Similarly, there are no rules governing what gets linked to what.

---

[1] The term 'hypermedia' is a more general term than 'hypertext' and suggests that links exist to information held on different media. Both terms refer to a system of linked information, but 'hypermedia' looks set to be as mis-used as the previously fashionable 'multimedia'. We will therefore use the term 'hypertext' to refer to any document with such properties irrespective of the media which contain it. In the same way that the general term 'a text' refers to documents which may also contain 'graphics', so we shall use 'a hypertext' as a generic term to denote a document which may in fact be distributed across several media.

What makes hypertext different, what sets it apart from the most conceptually inter-linked paper document, is that in hypertext the links are 'machine-supported'. When the reader selects a hypertext link, the 'movement' between the two nodes takes place automatically. It is for this reason that the advent of hypertext has had to wait for the combination of processing power and display embodied in the modern computer.

For example, the screen shown in Figure 1 displays a hypertext concerning music. The 'top' level (obscured in this view by overlapping windows) offers the user a view of music organised by instrument, composer, historical time-line or geographical location. In this case, 'composer' has been chosen, and the composer Wolfgang Amadeus Mozart has been further chosen for investigation. From here the user can access films about Mozart, display and print out musical scores, listen to complete works, read a biography and so forth. Of course, all these are interlinked so that from listening to music it is possible to move to the score and vice versa. In the biography, when a particular piece of music is mentioned, selecting the (bold) text plays an extract of the piece. When the text says that Mozart was born in Salzburg, a map can be called up showing Austria and surrounding countries and marked with the birthplaces of other composers, any of which could then be selected. All this movement around the information is achieved by the user or reader selecting items on screen with a mouse or other pointing device. What previously would have entailed visits to various libraries, sound libraries and cinemas can now be achieved from the desktop.

This example serves to show how flexible the concepts of *node* and *link* are. A node of information can be a fragment of music, a piece of text, a map, a complete film — anything which the author thinks can sensibly be presented as a unit. Even if a particular hypertext system always displays one screenful of information at a time, a node can consist of several consecutive screens. Similarly, a link is arbitrary in the sense that there are no rules to say where a link shall be made. A link can be made between any two nodes which the author (or often the 'reader' as we shall see later) considers to be connected in some way. In some systems, the links are 'typed', i.e., there are several types of link and the author must specify which type he would like to make at any one time. For example, the system might limit links to those which connect information offering *support* for an argument, *refutation* of an argument, an *example* and so forth. However, many systems use untyped links. As we shall see in the chapter on authoring, the flexibility of the size of nodes and the positioning of links places a burden on the author and reader which many paper documents do not.

Various hypertext systems have implemented the simple ideas in different ways and hence superficially they might look quite different. They might even feel

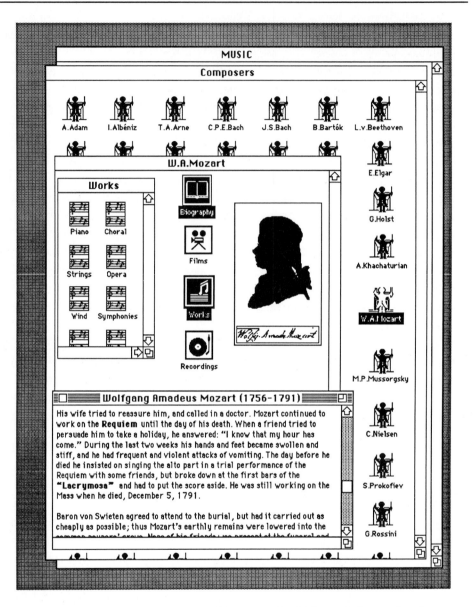

Figure 1: A music hypertext, with the life and work of Mozart being explored.

different to use. For example, selecting a link may cause an overlapping window containing the linked text to open, or it may replace the node with the linked node. Similarly, replacing a node with a linked node may be couched in terms of 'unfolding' or of physical jumping between nodes. However, there is sufficient similarity between the different systems to allow their grouping under the heading of 'non-linear text', 'dynamic documentation', or hypertext.

The fact that links are supported electronically is insufficient to define a system as hypertext. For example, database management systems (DBMSs) have links of various kinds, notably relational and object-oriented links. It might be possible to build a free-form relational database resembling a hypertext database, but such systems usually emphasise 'selection against criteria' and 'reporting' rather than reading and browsing.

Similarly, the inverted file common in information management systems (IMSs) could be seen as a set of links allowing any word to be accessed. However, in such systems a word is simply an alphanumeric string, the basis for a search operation rather than a unit of meaning. A sophisticated system will allow the user (or, more typically, the 'database administrator') to define synonyms in terms of links between equivalent terms in the inverted file, and a thesaurus of words and phrases arranged according to their meaning could be constructed with the inverted file terms as the base level. However, the operation is still essentially one of searching rather than linking on the basis of meaning.

With both the DBMS and the IMS it is possible to build a database which ostensibly resembles hypertext, so why are such constructions not *really* hypertext? What differs is the underlying purpose for which such systems were designed, and consequently the effort involved in producing such a database and supporting changes to it. The situation is analogous to a graphics package with a text facility; such a package could be used to produce a paper document indistinguishable from the output of a word processing package, but the effort required is related to the purpose for which the package was designed. You *could* write letters with a drawing package, but you *wouldn't*.

Why is hypertext important?

There are many developments taking place in research laboratories each year, so why should hypertext be seen as important enough to merit the attention it is receiving? Its importance is based on the fact that it offers a very powerful way of organising and accessing information and hence has a potential rôle to play in the development of information technology, which in turn is shaping the society in which we live. If we look at the period from 1961 to 1981, there was a strong growth in both information occupations and information industries. The greatest growth was exhibited by information occupations in information industries, followed by non-information occupations in information industries, followed by information occupations in non-information industries. The fourth group, non-information occupations in non-information industries, experienced a consistent and accelerating decrease in percentage of job opportunities over this period. Projections of future employment made on the basis of these trends show a continuing move away from manufacturing industry towards services, especially services with an information content (Angell, 1987).

An increase in information work, coupled with an increased use of communication technology, could lead to wide-ranging changes in society. Following the Industrial Revolution, many towns developed around sources of power such as coal mines and rivers. With more people able to work remote from an office, there is a decreasing need for populations to build up in towns. As demographic factors such as dwelling patterns change, so too does the nature of society. Patterns of interaction change and the style of life changes. These changes permeate through society affecting, for example, the kinds of crime committed. Computer-related crimes are now commonplace, ranging from large-scale fraud to 'hacking' of Prince Philip's electronic mail.

Hypertext's importance resides in the fact that it may alter the way in which we read, write and organise information. As we will suggest in Chapter 2, these skills have supported the technical advances of the last 3000 years. Any powerful information access and retrieval mechanism will have potentially wide-ranging effects, and these will extend beyond the office into the school and even the home.

Of course, some of the claims made for hypertext need careful consideration. For example, it has been claimed that hypertext will change the way we think. In a modified version of such a claim, Beeman *et al.* (1987) suggest that education is about the development of "non-lineal" thinking and that hypertext assists in the development of this style of thinking. We will consider the rôle which hypertext can play in education in Chapter 6. Marchionini and Shneiderman (1988) echo this view when they say that "the application of computers as cognitive augmenting agents will improve cognitive performance and change the way we think." For these authors, hypertext systems are "the next generation of word processing" which will change the way people read and write. Any such claims must of course be subjected to experimental testing, and we will review many experimental findings in later chapters.

Hypertext historical highlights

Rather than indulge in historical oneupmanship — who knows, maybe the scratchings around the cave paintings were the first primitive hypertext links? — we will begin our brief overview of the history of hypertext in the same era as the birth of the technology which supports it. The article most often cited as the birthplace of hypertext is Vannevar Bush's "As we may think" (Bush, 1945). The link between hypertext and thought implied in the title of Bush's article is an interesting question which we will address in more detail in Chapter 6.

Bush was appointed the first director of America's Office of Scientific Research and Development by President Roosevelt in 1941. He saw clearly the problems associated with ever-increasing volumes of information:

> "There is a growing mountain of research. But there is increased evidence that we are being bogged down today as specialization extends. The investigator is staggered by the findings and conclusions of thousands of other workers — conclusions which he cannot find time to grasp, much less to remember, as they appear. Yet specialization becomes increasingly necessary for progress, and the effort to bridge between disciplines is correspondingly superficial."

Presented with an extract such as this, it surprises many people to discover that the author was writing 45 years ago, since many contemporary writers have made exactly the same point about the 'information explosion'.

To cope with this plethora of information, Bush designed (conceptually, at least) the 'memex', a device "in which an individual stores his books, records, and communications, and which is mechanized so that it may be consulted with exceeding speed and flexibility." More than a simple repository, the memex was based on "associative indexing, the basic idea of which is a provision whereby any item may be caused at will to select immediately and automatically another. This is the essential feature of the memex. The process of tying two items together is the important thing."

For Bush, 'tying two items together' was important because it seemed to him to follow the workings of the mind, which

> "…operates by association. With one item in its grasp, it snaps instantly to the next that is suggested by the association of thoughts, in accordance with some intricate web of trails carried by the cells of the brain."

In view of the way we described the essential features of hypertext earlier, it is not difficult to see why Bush is often regarded as its founding father.

In conception, the memex was a remarkable 'scholar's workstation' and Bush thought that it would allow a new form of publishing, with documents "ready-made with a mesh of associative trails running through them, ready to be dropped into the memex and there amplified." Unfortunately for a visionary like Bush, the technology of the day was not up to the task of instantiating the memex. He assumed that microfilm would cope with the bulk of the storage problem, which might have been true. However, the level and complexity of indexing and retrieval required by the memex was certainly beyond microfilm-based technology. The memex was a problem in search of a solution, and the solution was the computer.

The one thing which Bush did not do was to name this nascent field of endeavour. The term 'hypertext' is attributed to Theodor (Ted) Nelson, a character who 25 years after coining the term can still hold an audience's attention with his vision of how the future of literature might look. Nelson's Xanadu project — characteristically named after the site of Kubla Khan's pleasure dome in Coleridge's poem — is aimed at the creation of a 'docuverse', a structure in which the entire literature of the world is linked, a "universal instantaneous hypertext publishing network" (Nelson, 1988).

In Xanadu, nothing ever needs to be written twice. A document is built up of original (or 'native') bytes and bytes which are 'inclusions' from other documents in which they are themselves native. By the Summer of 1989, Nelson had moved from speaking of 'inclusions' to speaking of 'transclusions', a term which implies the transfer and inclusion of part of one document into another. However, an important aspect of Xanadu is that the transclusion is virtual, with each document containing links to the original document rather than copies of its parts.

It could be argued that someone who speaks of a docuverse, xanalogical structure and transclusions should not be surprised that his project is "not well understood." However, Nelson continues to work towards his vision, publishing details of the 'humber' system for keeping track of the large number of documents in the docuverse (Nelson, 1988) and distributing flysheets announcing the imminent availability of the Xanadu Hypermedia Information Server software.

Although Nelson is seen as one of the gurus or Grand Old Men of hypertext, the idea of much of the world's literature being connected had been suggested many years previous. At a talk given in 1936 (and subsequently published in 1938), almost ten years before even Bush's article, the British writer and visionary H G Wells had described his idea of a World Encyclopædia, the organisation of which would:

> "...spread like a nervous network...knitting all the intellectual workers of the world through a common interest and a common medium of expression into a more and more conscious co-operating unity."

In a world which was about to be embroiled in the greatest war ever, Wells's article can be seen as a plea for thinking people to work together in peace. Modern political theorists might now judge the article to be naïve, but the practicalities — including issues like copyright which Wells foresaw — are still being worked on today in the field of hypertext.

Nelson may have given hypertext its name but he was by no means the only person working on the ideas. Although perhaps better known as the inventor of the mouse pointing device and the five-key 'chording' keyboard, Doug Engelbart has been pursuing his vision of hypertext since the early 1960s. Engelbart's emphasis has always been on augmenting or amplifying human intellect, a fact now reflected in the naming of his system as Augment. His original proposal was for a system he called H-LAM/T — Human using Language, Artifacts and Methodology, in which he is Trained — although the first implementation had the simpler title of NLS — oN Line System. NLS was meant as an environment to serve the working needs of Engelbart's Augmented Human Intellect Research Centre at Stanford Research Institute, a computer-based environment containing all the documents, memos, notes, reports and so forth but also supporting planning, debugging and communication. As such, NLS can be seen as one of the earliest attempts to provide a hypertext environment in which computer-supported collaborative work could take place, a development which will be discussed in more detail in Chapter 8.

We can see Bush, Nelson and Engelbart as representing three different views of hypertext which continue to attract adherents today. The Bush view sees hypertext as somehow 'natural', reflecting the mind or (in the strongest form of this position) modeling the mind; from this perspective, hypertext should feel easy to use. The Engelbart view of hypertext is as an augmentation environment; the user of hypertext should be able to achieve more than would be possible without it. Although Nelson's vision is perhaps the most ambitious, his view of hypertext is as a storage and access mechanism; the user of hypertext should be able to access any document, and such ease of access should work to break down subject boundaries.

These views are not mutually exclusive; it is possible to advocate a hypertext system which provides ready access to all information and therefore allows users to perform new tasks. Indeed, there is a fine line between these idealised positions and it is not always possible to describe any particular system (or system designer's viewpoint) in terms of one or any of them. However, the fact that different views can proliferate illustrates the point that 'hypertext' is not a unitary concept, not a single thing which can be defined any more precisely than in terms of nodes and links. It is for this reason that hypertext software packages with completely different 'look and feel' can be produced and still claim to embody the concept of hypertext.

Although many hypertext systems have been developed since the pioneering work of Nelson and Engelbart, it is not our intention to describe them all in this chapter. Conklin (1987) lists 18 systems and his list is not complete if for no other reason than because others have been developed since his article was written. Rather, we will now move to the end of the chain leading from mainframe to microcomputer and mention only two other people who seem to us to be important for various reasons.

Randall Trigg is credited with the first PhD thesis on hypertext (Trigg, 1983) in which he describes a system called Textnet. However, Trigg has had a greater impact on the field of hypertext since he moved to the Xerox Palo Alto Research Centre where he was one of the developers of the NoteCards system (Halasz, Moran and Trigg, 1987). NoteCards was designed as an information analyst's support tool, one which would aid the analyst in forming better conceptual models and analyses. As its name suggests, the system implements in electronic form the well-known index or note card much used by information workers, and extends the metaphor to include the FileBox (traditionally a shoe-box).

The main factor which has limited the use of NoteCards is that it requires the use of an expensive Xerox Lisp computer. Even so, it has been used as a research tool in several application areas, with Trigg also exploring its use as an environment in which to perform computer supported collaborative working (Trigg and Suchman, 1989). However, possibly the biggest impact which NoteCards has had has been indirect; like several other aspects of the work at Xerox PARC, it has influenced Apple Computer and can be seen as the model for Apple's HyperCard. Today HyperCard is the most widely distributed hypertext system and consequently the best known and most used.

Unfortunately, while HyperCard has served to introduce the word *hypertext* into many peoples' vocabulary, it has also been responsible for giving many of these people a wrong impression. HyperCard is a powerful tool, one which can do more than produce hypertext documents. It has an important use as a rapid prototyping tool and even an application generator — it has been called 'the programming environment for the rest of us' echoing Steve Jobs' description of the Macintosh as 'the computer for the rest of us.' Hence, some people have assumed that the context of hypertext is sufficiently all-embracing as to include such things as the fully functional mobile phone simulation built in HyperCard by some of the authors' colleagues at the HUSAT Research Institute. It is a mistake to think that everything produced using HyperCard is hypertext or, conversely, that all hypertext systems have the same properties as HyperCard.

The movement from research laboratory to commercial software venture is one which has not been made very often. However, the Guide hypertext system currently available commercially for the Apple Macintosh and IBM PC, can claim to have made the transition with some success. The system has been the subject of research and development by Peter Brown and colleagues at the University of Kent since 1982, but in 1984 Office Workstations Ltd (OWL) became interested and have since developed the microcomputer versions. The original system, still the focus of research at Kent, runs under the Unix operating system.

Unlike many systems which use the card metaphor or present information a screen at a time (like pages), Guide uses a scrolling method similar to word processors. Indeed, a Guide document is presented as a single scrolling field. Within the text are 'buttons' which, when selected, are replaced by the associated text. For example, Figure 2 shows a screen from a journal article held in Guide format; when the word 'Introduction' is selected, the text is unfolded from behind the button as in Figure 3. Clicking on the text causes it to be re-folded behind the button. A read-only version of Guide has been used to distribute at least two books to date: the proceedings of the First UK Hypertext conference (McAleese, 1989b) and Ted Nelson's *Literary Machines*. To the best of our knowledge, the book which has *only* been distributed in hypertext form has yet to arrive. However, the concept of *hyperfiction* has been discussed (Howell, 1990), and short stories have been distributed in hypertext format (e.g., Engst's (1989) *Descent into the Maelstrom*), so it may be only a matter of time before an original hyperbook appears.

Many more hypertext systems exist and will continue to be developed in various centres around the world, including the USSR where the Hyperlog system has been

```
 ⌐  🍎  File  Edit  Search  Display  Format  Font  Size  Make       ¬
┌─────────────────────────────────────────────────────────────────┐
│▤□▥▥▥▥▥▥▥▥▥▥ Adrianson & Hjelmquist ▥▥▥▥▥▥▥▥▥▥□▤│
├─────────────────────────────────────────────────────────────────┤
│ Users' experiences of COM — a computer-mediated communication system  ▨│
│                                                                   ⇧│
│ LILLEMOR ADRIANSON and ERLAND HJELMQUIST                          │
│                                                                   │
│ Abstract                                                          │
│                                                                   │
│ 1. Introduction                                                   │
│                                                                   │
│ 2. Method                                                         │
│                                                                   │
│ 3. Results                                                        │
│                                                                   │
│ 4. Discussion                                                     │
│                                                                   │
│ Acknowledgment                                                    │
│                                                                   │
│ References                                                       ⇩│
│ |                                                                ▥│
└─────────────────────────────────────────────────────────────────┘
```

Figure 2: The top level of the article, where each heading is a 'button'.

⍽ File   Edit   Search   Display   Format   Font   Size   Make

═══════════════ **Adrianson & Hjelmquist** ═══════════════

Users' experiences of COM — a computer-mediated communication system

LILLEMOR ADRIANSON and ERLAND HJELMQUIST

Abstract

1. Introduction
    This study reports the results of a questionnaire given to users of
COM–a computer-mediated communication system. The COM system was
developed by the Swedish National Defence Research Institute and has been
used regularly since the beginning of 1979.
    COM is primarily a communication medium. It can be compared with a
gigantic notice-board (Palme 1979), which is accessible via terminals.
    The COM users communicate by typing into, and reading from, a
terminal. COM is organized into 'conferences', or meetings, on different
topics. Some of these conferences are work-related, others are seminar-like
and some take the form of informal 'social' discussions.
    Some of the unique capabilities provided by this kind of medium are

Figure 3: Selecting the 'Introduction' button causes the relevant text to be displayed.

developed. Several of them will be mentioned in ensuing chapters, with the
glossary containing brief details of the more important systems mentioned and a
reference to an original source if further information is required. Our aim in the
present chapter was not to list all known systems but rather to indicate the different
viewpoints which have led to the development of very different systems under the
umbrella of hypertext.

Overview of the book
In Chapter 2, we suggest that the significance of hypertext can only be assessed by
way of an appreciation of the historical development of text systems. We feel that
this perspective clearly reveals some popular conceptions concerning the linearity
of traditional text structures to be largely misconceived, and this in turn brings into
question some of the alleged advantages claimed for hypertext.
    Text systems have evolved considerably in terms of physical technology —
from papyrus to photo-typesetting — but this change is modest compared to the
change in our attitudes towards the rôle of writing. The evolution of the technology
and the cognitive skills of the users can be seen to be closely related to the the usage

of writing. Current hypertext systems do not appear to be capitalising on these hard-won skills.

Hypertext is not simply better or worse than paper documentation but it is different. In Chapter 3 we discuss the *usability* of hypertext by examining the users, their tasks and the texts from a psychological viewpoint. Drawing on the literature from psychology and ergonomics we demonstrate that in order to design a good hypertext system we need to address the interaction of the three elements of user, task and text.

To some people, navigation is the single biggest problem in hypertext, while others deny that such a problem exists. In Chapter 4 we address directly the problems of navigating through a complex information space. We review empirical evidence for the existence of the 'navigation problem' and, by drawing on psychological theories of navigation in physical environments, suggest how it might be lessened in the electronic domain.

The successful introduction of hypertext as a commonplace medium for organizing and accessing information will require the resolution of a number of practical and conceptual problems (in addition to the inevitable problems of standardisation and compatibility/interoperability). Many of the practical problems associated with creating hypertexts will prove to be less important as the transition to electronic information exchange progresses but the conceptual problems are less susceptible to technical solutions.

While the book as a medium has managed to support both searching and extended browsing successfully for some 500 years, this facility has declined as text length has increased. Contemporary technical texts may run to millions of pages and print is no longer a viable medium but although today's hypertext systems offer effective searching facilities, their support for browsing is often poor. Part of the problem results from the adoption of radical document architectures which place more emphasis on the computer's ability to support them than on the reader's ability to understand or make use of them. Traditional text structures are closely interrelated with our conceptions of intellectual argument and understanding of knowledge. Relatively unstructured hypertext networks would seem to be an inappropriate form for advanced teaching or learning but may prove a valuable tool for exploring and organizing information. We explore these issues in Chapter 5.

One of the areas in which hypertext might have far-reaching implications is that of education. Various claims have been made for the effectiveness of hypertext as a learning environment, and these claims are examined at length in Chapter 6 in the context of the educational process in general and the rôle of microcomputers in particular.

In Chapter 7 we describe the development of a hypertext database which embodies the design philosophy outlined in earlier chapters. The initial specification work and design decisions are outlined and users' responses to the interface are described.

Finally in Chapter 8 we outline the areas in which we think the future of hypertext lies and the areas to which research could be fruitfully directed.

CHAPTER TWO

LINEARITY AND HYPERTEXT

"As the art of reading (after a certain stage in one's education) is the art of skipping, so the art of being wise is the art of knowing what to overlook."
William James: The Principles of Psychology

The promise of hypertext?

Hypertext has been hailed as an invention of crucial importance because it offers radically new ways of structuring information. This advantage is in addition to those which result from the fact that hypertext is a form of electronic text, with all the possibilities this affords for flexible manipulation and rapid searching. For a field that is comparatively young, there is a surprising degree of unanimity concerning the characteristic which defines hypertext and offers this potential: it is simply the 'non-linearity' of the node and link structures of hypertexts. Hypertexts have been favourably compared to the supposedly fixed, linear formats of both paper-based and standard electronic texts (see, for example, Duncan, 1989; Cooke and Williams, 1989; Trigg and Irish, 1987; Beeman *et al.*, 1987.) Linear structures are typically seen as being constraining for both author and reader and an inferior way of presenting textual information. Duncan (1989) suggests that "a hypertext system can be both dynamic and interactive in a way that linear text can not — the user can explore a knowledge base in ways not previously determined by the system." Cooke and Williams (1989) claim that the aim of hypertext design should be to enable users "to explore information freely, in multiple parallel paths, instead of being confined to a fixed path or structure." The potential for user driven exploration is also echoed by Baird and Percival (1989).

These claims are comparatively modest compared to those of Beeman *et al.* (1987). They see the goal of higher education as being "the acquisition of a pluralistic cognitive style, which has an important property — non-lineality." This cognitive style is largely synonymous with "critical thinking", a style of thinking which encourages students "to see the world in inter-related relativistic terms rather than as isolated bits of information." For Beeman the paradox is that, although this is the goal, it is approached through "lineal communication, presentation and instruction". Linearity (or, rather, non-linearity) is therefore a central aspect of both the thinking behind hypertext and its practical applications.

In summary, it is widely claimed that hypertext represents a significant advance because it provides a means of representing knowledge which is not 'constrained' by the traditional 'linear' form of print technology. Furthermore, this new mode of representation, in addition to greatly facilitating information access, may enable ways of thinking which are pluralistic rather than sequential. In this chapter we shall consider whether linearity is an inherent property of written texts, whether this is a 'constraint' that needs to be overcome and finally the possible impact of hypertext systems. The possible impact of hypertext on education, learning and thinking is considered in Chapter 6, and alternative 'non-linear' texts are discussed in Chapter 3.

Linearity

A consideration of the physical characteristics of writing has led many people to the firm opinion that written texts are inherently linear and therefore constrained in the way that they can represent knowledge (which is assumed to have a non-linear structure). However, a more sophisticated analysis of the way that written language is actually used reveals aspects that are definitely non-linear, and hence the idea of constraint seems unimportant or even inappropriate.

Linguistics differentiates human languages from other sign systems because they are linear, arbitrary, segmented and systematic. The concept of linearity has been uncritically accepted by non-linguists when discussing the characteristics of spoken and written language. The arrival of hypertext with its non-linear, modular, semantic structure has encouraged many proponents to claim that this new medium can loosen constraints on the way ideas are presented, accessed and even conceived. This last claim is the most ambitious since it assumes a direct relationship between the linearity of language — and in particular that of the printed book — and the way that we construct arguments as linear chains of cause and effect. This tendency is seen as a distinct limitation because either (a) we think associatively rather than linearly and there is 'poor fit' between tool and user, or, (b) the technology serves us badly because it obliges us to think linearly (univariate, cause and effect) when the world is composed of complex multi-variate interactions.

The above arguments are unsound because not only are the conclusions debatable but the premise is also questionable. Human communication is an incredibly complicated technology, or set of interlinked technologies, with contrasting surface and underlying structural qualities. This is readily seen when the concept of linearity is considered. Speech is certainly linear in the most obvious respect since it is produced and heard chronologically and instantaneously. Words are uttered in sequence and the sound disappears almost immediately; thus in this respect the medium is uni-dimensional, and in everyday usage there is no enduring record outside of human memory. However, a closer examination shows that many of the underlying structures of oral communications are rarely linear and this, paradoxically, is also a result of the transitory nature of speech. In oral communication, meaning is constructed in an iterative fashion with much repetition because of the limitations of human memory — a fact that becomes very clear when conversations are transcribed.

Early writing systems were initially conceived of as means of recording human speech, as transcripts, and shared many of the surface characteristics of speech. However, as writing developed as a separate technology its characteristics were shaped by the fact that any written communication endures over time and is represented in two-dimensional graphical space. Although written language also appears highly linear because words are typically represented as sequences of discrete units, these units are fixed in two dimensional space in successive rows or columns. An example of a 'written' form which is obviously non-linear is the table. A table utilises the possibilities of two-dimensional display in order to convey concepts such as similarity, order, distinction and hierarchical classification. There is no inherent linear order to the way that information is extracted from a table. At a more general level, few books of any kind are read, or even written, linearly (as we will see in Chapter 5).

Linearity can thus be seen to be a characteristic of the media of spoken and written language but not of the messages that they convey. The present chapter will attempt to untangle this apparently contradictory position by examining the impact of literacy on the conception and transmission of knowledge. This overview will allow the proposed 'non-linearity' of hypertext to be considered in a wider context.

A review of the technologies developed to organise information (speech, writing, printing) suggests that although printing had an important influence on the way we regard and use visually organised information, the way we currently 'think' may be largely a product of the development and, to borrow McLuhan's (1962) term, 'interiorization' of alphabetic writing. The position is described concisely by Scribner and Cole (1981):

"As literacy shapes culture, the argument goes, so it shapes human minds.

A simple version of this argument appeals to the growth of the mind that results from the assimilation of knowledge and information transmitted by written texts. More radical is the claim that mastery of a written language affects not only the content of thought but also the process of thinking — *how* we classify, reason, remember." (p.5)

Orality and literacy — the medium shapes the message

The argument outlined above suggests an intimate and interactive relationship between the tools that we have as a species (i.e., first spoken and then written language) for expressing ideas and the nature of the ideas that are expressed. If this suggestion can be justified then the bolder assertion that hypertext may shape the nature of our conceptions becomes tenable. Hypertext might then be seen as both the next stage in the evolution of communications technology and the possible agent of a further increase in our intellectual and technological sophistication.

Anybody reading this book is likely to find it difficult to even conceive of an oral world that is not some variant of a literate world since the way that we think, and even our thoughts, have been shaped by literacy. However, by drawing evidence from a variety of perspectives, an understanding of oral modes of thought and expression is possible. An understanding of orality allows us to step outside our current literate perspective and thereby appreciate the impact of first script and then print on the organisation of knowledge.

The oral organisation of knowledge

At the beginning of this century, Milman Parry demonstrated that the Odyssey and Iliad contain a limited and repeated number of themes and were constructed from a library of well used expressions or clichés (see Parry, 1971). Subsequently, Lord (1960) showed that this is equally characteristic of contemporary oral epic poetry. This seemed anathema to many classical scholars — who considered the Homeric epics to be among the *literary* prizes of classical Greek culture — but these characteristics were inevitable when oral poetry's generation and perpetuation are considered. The Iliad and Odyssey are a unique, written insight into the oral tradition which lasted from the fall of Troy (c1250 BC) until the emergence of the Greek alphabet in about 750 BC, but Homer is nearly as mythical a figure as Odysseus.[1]

---

[1] "That there was an epic poet called Homer and that he played the primary part in shaping the Iliad and the Odyssey — so much may be said to be probable." *Encyclopædia Britannica Macropædia*, vol. 20, p. 695.

The Homeric epics may have been 'fixed' when writing was newly available but they are the product of a period when knowledge was transmitted via word of mouth and preserved only in human memory. According to Havelock (1963):

> "The only possible verbal technology available to guarantee the preservation and fixity of transmission was that of the rhythmic word organised cunningly in verbal and metrical patterns which were unique enough to retain their shape."

Thus the second 'intellectual' technology, following the development of language, was mnemonics — the art of memory. Ong (1982) summarises the techniques used by the oral epic poets:

> "In a primary oral culture, to solve effectively the problem of retaining and retrieving carefully articulated thought, you have to do your thinking in mnemonic patterns, shaped for ready oral recurrence. Your thought must come into being in heavily rhythmic, balanced patterns, in repetitions or antitheses, in alliterations and assonances, in epithetic and other formulary expressions, in standard thematic settings (the assembly, the meal, the duel, the hero's 'helper', and so on), in proverbs which are constantly heard by everyone so that they come to mind readily and which themselves are patterned for retention and ready recall, or in other mnemonic form. Serious thought is intertwined with memory systems."
> (p.34)

The epic poem is typically a series of episodes which are centred around individual experience. The perspective is usually subjective and the events are emotional and dramatic. As Chaytor (1945) puts it:

> "The unlettered audience cannot be treated tenderly; points must be vigorously emphasised; statements must be repeated, variety of diction must be introduced. The story-teller will present his characters in person, in conversation with each other, and by change of voice, intonation and gesture will make them live in the minds of his hearers, he must be something of an actor as well as a narrator." (p.55)

With the gift of hindsight this view of oral performance seems obvious. Even for highly literate audiences of today, the way in which a speech is made, be it dramatic monologue, formal address or traditional story, is crucial for its success; only a trivial part of the the actor's craft is concerned with learning the lines. If this is true today then it must have been of even greater significance when memory and speech were the only devices available for preserving and disseminating knowledge.

Since oral expression relied on human memory so completely for its preservation, it should not be difficult to see why the expressions were clichéd, repetitive, thematic, subjective and experiential. The same qualities are characteristic of the vehicle that oral cultures traditionally use to reflect their views of the world and its workings — mythology.

Plato was among the first to appreciate the possible impact that literacy would have on Greek thought and expression. Only a small proportion of the ten volumes of *The Republic* are given over to statecraft, while a relatively large proportion are devoted to a critical review of contemporary Greek education, art and philosophy. Among his principal targets were the poets, and he went as far as to advocate their exclusion from his 'Ideal State' because 'poetry cripples the intellect of the listeners'. Plato claimed that art and poetry appealed to the lower, less rational, part of human nature since they dealt primarily with the appearance of things. The following dialogue from Book 10 summarises his position:

> "The apparent size of an object, as you know, varies with its distance from our eye."
> "Yes"
> "So also a stick will look bent if you put it in the water, straight when you take it out, and differences of shading can make the same surface seem to the eye concave or convex; and it's clearly all a matter of our mind being confused. It is on this natural weakness of ours that the scene-painter and conjuror and their fellows rely when they deceive us with their tricks."
> "True."
> "Measuring, counting and weighing were invented to help us out of these difficulties, and to ensure that we should not be guided by apparent differences of size, quantity and heaviness, but by proper calculations of number, measurement, and weight — calculations which can only be performed by the element of reason in the mind."

Plato saw not only that the domination of poetry had to be broken to allow prose to develop, but that the oral mode of thought which had generated the poetic tradition would also have to be abandoned. This would be necessary if scientific rationalism with its implied analysis and classification of experience and rearrangement into sequences of cause and effect were to become a common mode of thought. It should be remembered that it was not only 'art' that was preserved in poetic form but any enduring cultural activity: commerce, history, education, law and civil or religious custom.

The character of writing

Many of McLuhan's assertions concerning the deterministic nature of communication media are based on the fact that the Greek alphabet was an abstract, linear code in which atomistic units were assembled to make semantically meaningful messages.[2] However, there are also important consequences resulting from the introduction of writing that are revealed from a higher level analysis; from the fact that it supports remote, asynchronous communication with a permanent record. The asynchronous aspect of written communication contributes to its detached and objective character. A written text is prepared in advance of its delivery and can be endlessly revised until the precise form intended by the author is reached, without the reader being aware of this process. This has resulted in a concern with exactitude of meaning and tone which is rarely appropriate with oral forms of expression. In stark contrast, oral performers who repeatedly correct themselves will appear less, not more, authoritative.

A speaker and listener, or audience, not only share a common physical context but the speaker can also make assumptions regarding the prior knowledge, or previous experience, of the audience. In contrast, the writer must ensure that his message is completely self contained in terms of information content and cannot rely on direct feedback from the audience or any other type of external support.

As a simple example, consider the situation in which an 'expert' is describing the operation of a piece of sophisticated machinery to a group of potential new users. He can not only use gesture to indicate particular features and determine whether the audience is attending to them but he can also engage in a dialogue to achieve further clarity. Additionally, the speaker can make assumptions about the audience's previous experience and tailor the verbal explanation accordingly. The author of technical documentation is well advised to write so that as wide an 'audience' as possible can obtain all the information they require from the text, but this is not without risk — there is a danger of creating a text which, in attempting to be appropriate to every reader, is in fact appropriate to no one. (Admittedly the readers have the advantage of being able to re-read the text as often as they wish and they may well be able to inspect technical drawings.)

It was not merely a useful characteristic of writing that it could be explicit, rather than implicit, in its conveyance of meaning; it was an inherent property. Although the first texts were written recordings of oral statements (e.g., the Homeric epics), the potential of the writing for 'prose form' was gradually realised. Havelock (1980) ascribes this change to the preservative power of writing:

---

2   Previous 'alphabets' had been much less abstract. They had used characters to represent syllables rather than sounds, which inevitably leads to much larger character sets (see Havelock, 1980).

"Vocabulary and syntax had been controlled by the pressure to memorize. This limited anything that was said to what could be said rhythmically, and in narrativized form, meaning actions performed by agents which happened to them. Even the wording of what is more easily recognizable as preserved wisdom—the maxim, aphorisms, parables, and proverbs— had to conform to these laws. Once the same speech is placed in documented form, the pressure to memorise is relieved, though not at first abolished. The document can lie around available for re-reading and re-consultation without prior necessity of oral recall. Therefore the pressures for poetry as a preservative, and for a restriction to narrative syntax, are relieved also. The twin possibilities exist of a preserved prose, and a prose which no longer tells a story. It can allow itself to express other types of discourse." (p.96)

The written text eventually came to be autonomous, and readers and authors expected it to 'stand alone.' As Olson (1977) puts it, in oral discourse 'the meaning is in the context', while in contrast, in literate tradition, 'the meaning is in the text'. Explicit text allowed the formulation and preservation of statements that could not only be counter to the reader's previous experience or 'common sense' but could also be subject to critical analysis. This enabled a concern about 'literal truth'; the separation of mythology and history (Herodotus); and the development of systems of logical inference through analysis of the relationships among statements (Aristotle). Writing is also a medium which supports private study rather than the communal organisation represented by a teacher addressing, and being questioned by, his students (e.g., Socrates). A text designed for private study will need to be self explanatory since there will be no opportunity to interrogate the author. In contrast, Olson (1977) points out that:

"Oral language statements must be poetized to be remembered, but in the process they lose some of their explicitness; they require interpretation by a wise man, scribe, or cleric." (p.263)

Until now we have considered the impact of literacy in a historical context and, however convincing the argument, most of the evidence is indirect — by definition, oral cultures leave no permanent record. Fortunately, an alternative approach is possible because literacy, even today, is not a universal experience.

Contemporary perspectives on literacy
As Scribner and Cole (1981) point out, the fundamental changes in modes of

thinking associated with literacy have all been inferred on the basis of changes at the cultural and linguistic level. There has been comparatively little effort to determine whether contemporary non-literate individuals or societies think or conceive of the world in ways which differ from literate individuals or societies. This objection betrays an element of simplification over the distinction of literacy/non-literacy. It is possible to think of a society which is wholly oral composed of members which are non-literate or pre-literate.[3] In a society which has minority groups in which literacy is rare, it is not entirely appropriate to consider their members as being unaffected by literacy. There are many ways in which the ideas, concepts and structures generated by literacy will have affected their lives and in turn may shape their cognitive processes.

However, with this caveat in mind, a small number of investigations have shown striking differences in the modes of thinking of oral and literate individuals. The most notable of these is probably the one undertaken by Alexander Luria, a Russian psychologist who gathered data in two remote Russian provinces (Uzbekistan and Kirghizia) during the period 1931–2. The aim of the research was to investigate the impact of the socio-economic and cultural changes resulting from the revolution on the cognitive development of individuals living in the less developed regions. Striking differences were found between the non-literate and those with only a moderate degree of literacy. The non-literate peasants appeared incapable of demonstrating abstract reasoning or formal logic and they apparently conceived of the world in familiar, concrete ways.

In one of Luria's tests, the subjects were presented with drawings of four objects (a hammer, hatchet, log and saw) and were asked to group the objects according to their similarity. The literate and semi-literate subjects invariably placed the tools together in a single category with the log separate, while the non-literate did not appear to employ categorical thinking at all: to them, all four objects are intimately related. As Ong (1982) suggests:

> "If you are a workman with tools and see a log, you think of applying the tool to it, not of keeping the tool away from what it was made for — in some weird intellectual game." (p.51)

This operational, or 'real-life', mode of thought is beautifully captured in the reply of a 25 year old illiterate:

> "They're all alike. The saw will saw the log and the hatchet will chop it into small pieces. If one of these has to go, I'd throw out the hatchet. It doesn't do as good a job as the saw." (Luria, 1976, p 56)

---

3   Illiteracy can only occur in a context where literacy is the norm.

Luria also attempted to determine the peasants' capacity to employ formal deductive logic — a Greek invention that appeared after the adoption of the alphabet. The non-literate peasants' responses to simple syllogisms revealed a marked tendency to reject the self-contained and arbitrary premises in favour of real life knowledge, as though they were answering a riddle. Thus in response to the syllogism *'In the Far North, where there is snow, all bears are white. Novaya Zembla is in the far North and there is always snow there. What colour are the bears?'* a typical response was, 'I don't know. I've seen a black bear. I've never seen any others... Each locality has its own animals.' (Luria, 1976, p.108). However, a semi-literate 45-year-old replied 'To go by your own words, they should all be white.' (Luria, 1976, p.114). The respondent produces the 'correct' reply but is dubious about the premises since they are not in accord with his own experience.

It has been suggested that written expression is, by nature, objective and detached compared to spoken language and that this characteristic enables an abstract perspective. Without accepting the technological determinism implied by this argument, it is undeniable that in current everyday usage language differs markedly depending on whether it is spoken or written. While written text is continuous, natural oral utterances have been found to be produced in spurts of about two seconds duration and six words in length. William James (1950) suggested this represented a single 'perching' of consciousness and later psychologists have seen this as reflecting a limitation of cognitive processing.[4]

According to Chafe (1982), when we come to write "we have time to integrate a succession of ideas into a single linguistic whole in a way that is not available in speaking" (p.37). Chafe describes a revealing study in which verbal statements from the same individuals produced in oral and written contexts that varied in formality (dinner table conversations, lectures, private correspondence and academic papers) were compared. The oral samples were found to be composed of idea units linked with co-ordinating conjunctions (*and, but, so, because*, etc.) while the written samples contained examples of a variety of techniques for integrating associated, subordinate, or qualifying ideas into what would have been a single utterance in an oral delivery. The oral construction of complex units such as these is usually achieved only by those considered highly articulate (and that usually means literate). The written samples were also found to be much more likely to include use of the 'passive voice' — a device usually employed to distance the speaker from the subject being described. Similarly, the written material was less likely to contain first person references (*I, we, my*, etc.), references to the

---

4   See, for example, Miller (1956) and the concept of 'chunking'.

speaker's mental processes (*I felt...*, *I thought...*, etc.), fuzziness (*sort of*, *about*, *lots of*, etc.), expressions of enthusiastic involvement (*really good*) and direct quotes (*and then he said "..."*). Thus, oral language has a tendency to fragmentation and involvement while written texts are more inclined to integration and detachment.

So far, we have considered the nature of oral communication and modes of thought and then looked at the way that literacy changes not only the ways in which things are said but also the way in which we think. We have seen this in both historical and contemporary contexts and related this to the inherent characteristics of the media concerned. If hypertext represents a major change in representation technology, might it not seem highly likely that it will also have a significant impact on the form and content of our ideas? Before attempting to answer this question we shall turn to the second major theme of this chapter — the extent to which linearity in texts is a constraint that needs to be overcome. We shall see that, while manuscript technology may initially have been constrained and constraining, this limitation was gradually overcome.

The evolution of writing — from record to resource

The historical evolution of literacy and 'manuscript technology' clearly shows the relationship between linearity and text. While early texts were undoubtedly 'linear' in terms of content and usage, the increasing sophistication of both technology and readers' skills allowed this 'limitation' to be overcome. Indeed, in some respects it is possible to claim that the linear document was obsolete by the 13th century! In this light, the claims that hypertext has the potential to free the reader from the constraints of linear based documents appear to be unjustified.

In England, the origins of popular literacy can be traced to the centuries following the Norman invasion of 1066. A wealth of documentary evidence is available that gives a clear insight into both the important changes resulting from the availability of written records and increased literacy. It is all too easy to assume that the skills of reading and writing, and attitudes towards them, were much the same in the middle ages as they are today and this is far from true. The following quote from Clanchy (1979) suggests some of the practices required in an age when literacy was still restricted to an educated few while the population at large relied on oral memory:

> "In the summer of 1297 some jurors from Norfolk came to the court of King's Bench to attest that Robert de Tony was 21 years of age and was therefore entitled to have his wardship terminated. Proving the age of

feudal heirs by sworn testimony was a routine procedure, in which each juror attempted to recollect some memorable event which coincided with the birth of the child in question. Jurors might recall, for example, specific gifts or public events or accidents to themselves or their neighbours." (p.175)

The popular acquisition of writing during the late middle ages freed people from the need to memorise knowledge in order for it to be passed on to future generations, and freed knowledge from the requirement that it should be encoded in a form amenable to verbal memorisation — thus repeating a process that had transformed Greek society some 2000 years before. And, once again, writing made it possible for people to have objective knowledge of the world in addition to subjective knowledge:

> "writing fosters abstractions that disengage knowledge from the arena where human beings struggle with one another." (Ong, 1982, p 43).

Historians, like Clanchy, have tended to assume that prior to the Norman invasion there had been no significant evolution in the technology or practice of literacy since the demise of the Roman Empire some 500 years before. But although the document-based Norman administrative system significantly increased both the importance of literacy among lay circles and the stock of secular texts, the evolution of literacy and manuscript technology had begun much earlier.

The majority of written texts produced in the later Roman era were composed of continuous rows of upper-case characters without word gaps or punctuation — as was the common practice in earlier Greek inscriptions.[5] This style is entirely phonetic rather than ideographic. While Latin was the language of every day speech as well as erudite discourse, it could be read and written by very few — the educated elite. Writing was a process of transcription, with each successive sound being captured and given a permanent visual form. Spelling mistakes were often the result of mispronunciation by the writer/dictator but the reader was aided by the strong inflexion/conjugation and tightly-controlled sentence construction of Latin.

Words committed to paper were intended for reading aloud — indeed most texts were letters, decrees, proclamations and so forth, and were typically read aloud in their entirety, thus recreating the original oral form. Hence, even prose had a strong rhythmic quality, and writing was phonetically biased. According to Saenger (1982):

---

5   Roman inscriptions commonly used a point to separate words from a comparatively early period
     but this practice is missing in the Latin books of the 4th, 5th and 6th centuries AD.

"The Roman reader, reading aloud to others or softly to himself, approached the text syllable by syllable in order to recover the words and sentences conveying the meaning of the text...A written text was essentially a transcription which, like modern musical notation, became an intelligible message only when it was performed orally to others or to oneself." (p.371)

The virtual impossibility of rapid, visual and silent reading had a number of consequences. The scribe making copies was obliged to read short sections aloud and then write them down or to work with a dictator. The texts which were used as references required the use of marginal flags to provide access cues to specific items contained within the unbroken text. Quintilian, in a text on the art of rhetoric, recommended allocating marginal signs to specific arguments in a speech to be committed to memory. The signs were then to be memorised using visual-spatial techniques.

When the Christian church spread to the western fringes of Europe in the 6th century, it took with it Latin and literacy. However, according to Saenger (1982), while the Celts, for example, were converted to Christianity without too much difficulty, they experienced difficulty when reading Latin scriptures and liturgical texts aloud — they had no previous experience of literacy or everyday use of spoken Latin. In order to help pronunciation, it became common for words to be written with separations. Word spacing allowed the weaker reader to recognise complete words and reduced the need to build them up by verbally pronouncing their constituent sounds. This process was also facilitated by the gradual introduction of miniscule characters.[6] Word separation and a more distinctive set of characters enabled the transformation of reading from being a predominantly oral/aural activity to a visual one. An early consequence of this change was the development of visual transcription which allowed scribes to copy texts silently. However, while this may have silenced the mumblings that had previously been characteristic of the monastic scriptorium, reading outside remained largely oral. The requirement for more widespread silent, and consequently rapid, reading did not arise until a later period.

While literacy was preserved within the monasteries of Europe during the Dark Ages, faster reading offered no particular advantage since reading served largely liturgical and devotional needs. However, this changed radically following the rise of medieval scholasticism in the 12th century. Scholasticism was associated with a

---

6   Miniscule characters were smaller than the previous majuscule (capital like) style but had ascending and descending strokes (as in the contemporary lower case characters b, d, k and p, y, g). Miniscule characters provide much more distinctive word shapes compared to words composed of capital forms.

virtual information explosion of textual material:

> "University scholars needed to read faster to master the large and ever-growing corpus of glosses on Scripture and commentaries on cannon law which replaced letters and sermons as the preferred literary genre. Because of the greater freedom it afforded to movements of the eye, silent reading favored the perusal and reference consultation of books." (Saenger, 1982, p.385)

There was not just an increase in the volume of textual material; there was an equally significant increase in the complexity of the content. This exposed the limitations of oral styles of reading: complex arguments require detailed consideration with frequent re-view and are not well suited to being read aloud to an audience.

Scholasticism also radically changed the ways in which texts were created. Prior to this period, authors had typically dictated to the highly skilled scribe who first recorded the words on wax tablets of fairly limited capacity and then made a fair copy on vellum or parchment — a slow and laborious process. Scholars like Thomas Aquinas and Albert Magus preferred to compose their long and increasingly complex works on parchment directly using a cursive script. The description of text usage given by Saenger (1982) suggests that academic reading and writing styles have hardly changed in 600 years and that the concept of hypertext would have been as welcome then as it is to many scholars today:

> "Composition in the medium of quires and sheets of parchment meant that authors could revise and rearrange their texts while composing them. This facility aided thirteenth century scholastic writers to prepare texts rich in cross-references which presupposed that the reader, like the author, had the ability to flip from folio to folio in order to relate arguments to their logical antecedents and to compare comments on related but disparate passages of a Scripture." (p.386)

The presentation format of manuscripts evolved in a similar way over this period as their rôle changed from sacred devotional relics to sources of information to be studied visually and silently. In the early middle ages it was rare for text to be split into sections shorter than the chapter, and many manuscripts of the Old Testament were not even divided into chapters. During the later middle ages, not only were chapter divisions introduced into classical texts but sub-divisions were also added by university scholars. This enabled the construction of tables of chapter headings, running headings and alphabetical tables by subject to become standard features of academic text.

While manuscripts were often visually beautiful, this has often been mistakenly taken as some sort of evidence that they were of limited utility. The Domesday Book for example used vermilion paint for three different types of rubric — capital letters for the names of shires and other headings; shading for the initial letter of each paragraph and certain abbreviations; underlining for the names of places and tenants. In legal manuscripts letters of the alphabet were used in the margins to indicate relevant sections of the text and this system was later used to gloss literary texts. An even more remarkable example of manuscript craft and utility is the Canterbury Psalter produced *circa* 1147. On each page the calligrapher managed to display three versions of St Jerome's Latin text of the Psalms in parallel columns (see Figure 4) In addition, there are interlinear Latin glosses and Anglo-Saxon and French translations. If hypertext can have a paper format, this must represent its ultimate visual expression; it is difficult to imagine the usage of such a document as being 'constrained by the linear, paper-based format'.

The switch from oral to visual emphasis can also be seen in the increased importance of diagrammatic illustrations in the manuscripts of the late middle ages. The presence of diagrams in very early texts has been largely overlooked in favour of representational illustrations — which seems surprising since their origins apparently go back as far as Aristotle's works according to Saenger (1982), and they appear to suffer less corruption as a result of successive copying. However, diagrams achieved much greater prominence with the rise of scholasticism. The use of schematic diagrams in scholastic texts is significant since it clearly shows yet again how the written form managed to overcome the apparent restrictions of a fixed format. According to Evans (1980):

> "The essence of the scholastic method is the dialectical analysis of concepts. Thesis and antithesis are subjected to an examination (interrogatio) against empirical evidence and the evidence of established authorities (auctoritates). After a solution has been reached, the unacceptable arguments are refuted in turn. A necessary prelude to this is the division (distinctio) of concepts into their basic elements. The *distinctio* can be set out graphically on the page, so that a topic is visually analysed into its parts and sub-parts by interposing a stratified deployment of terms within the syntax of the sentence. ... It is no longer a page of text which can be read aloud with equal effect; it is a visual experience." (p.34)

Evans includes a page from a 14th century French manuscript to illustrate this point and his explanatory note gives a vivid impression of the figure's expressive power:

Figure 4 — the Canterbury Psalter

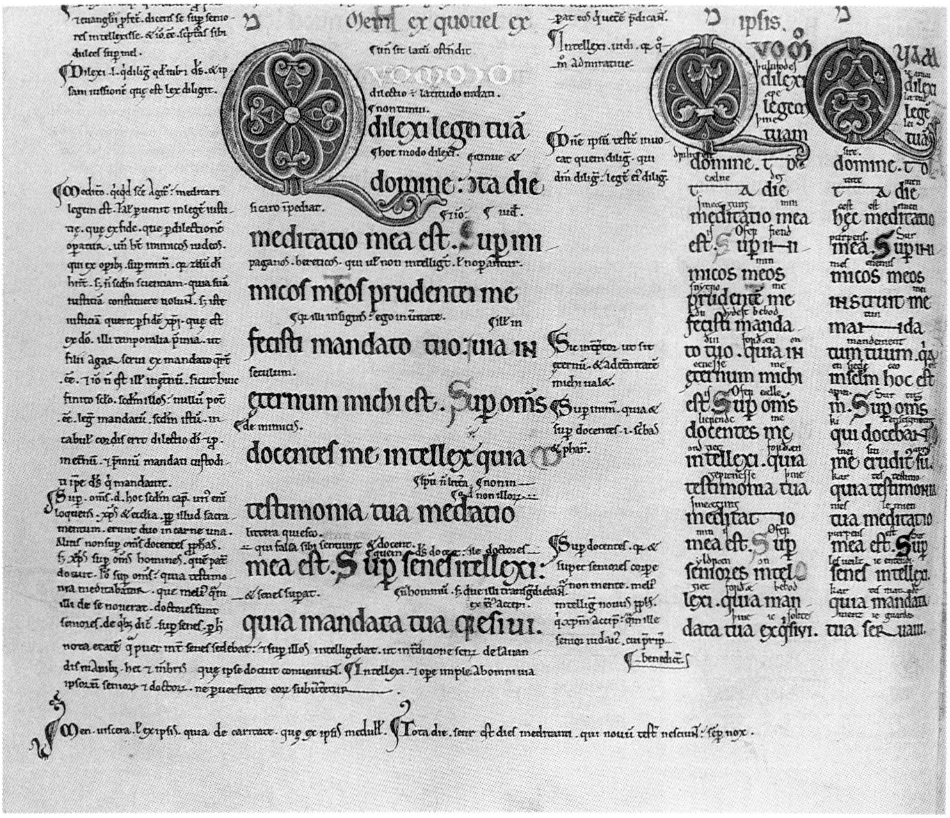

"The opening matter describes the division of the soul into three faculties, Intellect, Memory and Will, and explains how each of these qualities embodies the other two. The argument is presented graphically by interpolating superimposed phrases articulated by linear elements within the sentences. This enables several different ideas to be expressed simultaneously within a relatively simple syntactical structure." (p.53)

It was only a relatively small step to abandon continuous prose completely and represent the *distinctio* as a schematic diagram, e.g., a hierarchical classification with the concept successively broken down into sub-component terms. These abstract diagrams were often given figurative forms such as trees, ladders or wheels.

Clanchy (1979) contrasts the attitudes shown towards books and styles of reading before and after the Norman invasion. Before the invasion books and reading (and writing) were largely confined to monastic communities and monks were "expected to ruminate on a text which had been designated to them as a sacred task" since "books, with their precious and brightly illuminated words, were images which produced a state of mystical contemplation and understanding." In contrast, by the time of Edward I who ruled from 1272 to 1307, Dominican monks and lay Court clerks "like modern academics, required extensive libraries in which they could glance rapidly over a whole series of books, many of very recent authorship, in order to construct a wide-ranging argument."

However, early manuscripts were still regarded in highly personal terms by readers — as though they were some orator's words made flesh. John of Salisbury, writing in the mid 12th Century, claimed that:

"Fundamentally letters are shapes indicating voices. Hence they represent things which they bring to mind through the windows of the eyes. Frequently they speak voicelessly the utterances of the absent" (cited in Clanchy, 1979, p.201).

---

7 Figure 4 (opposite) : The Canterbury or Eadwine Psalter. [Trinity College Cambridge MS.R.17.1 lower portion of fo. 219b. Psalm 118. Date : c1147.]

"The layout makes it possible to show all on one page the three versions of St Jerome's Latin text of the Psalms, side by side in parallel columns, together with Latin glosses and Anglo-Saxon and French translations. The main text, the 'Gallican', is in the largest script towards the left of the page its marginal and interlinear glosses, in miniature and abbreviated script, comprise a commentary derived from the Church Fathers...The pair of slimmer columns on the right of the page show the 'Roman' and 'Hebrew' variant texts. Between the lines of the 'Roman' text is the Anglo Saxon translation, written in a style derived from insular miniscules, and between the lines of the 'Hebrew' is the French translation."

Clanchy (1979)

This feeling was supported by the hand-crafted nature of the object and the often rhetorical style of the content. In fact, the majority of manuscripts did not even have titles and were referred to by their 'incipits' or opening phrases. If a medieval reader was asked who had written a particular manuscript then he would probably have suggested that it was the scribe rather than the 'author' of the text. Notions of originality, copyright and plagiarism have largely appeared since the advent of printing. In manuscript culture, authors were often regarded more as reporters or collators of material from much earlier (Classical) times.

Ong (1982) claims that the use of titles was a major factor in altering the perception of books from "frozen utterances" to things or objects, since titles are a form of label. However, reading and writing in Medieval times had far more in common with speaking than they do today. Reading meant reading aloud for the majority of readers until comparatively recently and even literate individuals often preferred to have a letter or statement read aloud to them than to read it themselves. Reading aloud and dictation also allowed the non-literate to participate in the use of documents whilst they are excluded by today's silent reading and writing. Until quite recently, undergraduate students were supposed to spend their time 'reading for a degree' in a given subject. With our current literate perspective, this evokes images of many hours spent by the students in private study poring over text books and learned journals. In the middles ages the meaning was quite different. The students would spend a good deal of their time listening, and probably taking dictation, while the lecturers read the texts out aloud.

The printed book

In the same way that an appreciation of orality is difficult for contemporary literate cultures, so it is also difficult (albeit to a lesser extent) to empathise with the world of manuscripts rather than printed books. Eisenstein (1979) considers the impact of printing on European culture at length and observes:

> "In order to assess changes ushered in by printing, for example, we need to survey the conditions that prevailed before its advent. Yet the conditions of scribal culture can only be observed through a veil of print."
> (p.8)

Conventional wisdom has recognised the importance of the development of printing in mid 15th Century Europe from an early stage, and Francis Bacon's observation that:

> "We should note the force, effect, and consequences of inventions which

are nowhere more conspicuous than in those three which were unknown to the ancients, namely, printing, gunpowder, and the compass. For these three have changed the appearance and state of the whole world." (Francis Bacon, *Novum Organum*, Aphorism 129)

is frequently quoted as proof.[8] However, the significance of print technology is usually assumed to be connected with improved access to written knowledge, i.e., greatly increased literacy and plentiful supplies of relatively cheap texts. Although this is undoubtedly true, it has tended to obscure less obvious but equally important factors.

The advent of an ever-increasing range of clearly printed texts radically changed reading skills. The manuscript reader not only spent much less time reading but the choice of material was very restricted. Consequently the level of fluency achieved by the average reader would be considered modest by contemporary standards. Chaytor (1945) contrasts the contemporary reader's skills with those probably achieved by a medieval reader:

> "Nothing is more alien to medievalism than the modern reader, skimming the headlines of a newspaper and glancing down its columns to glean any point of interest, racing through the pages of some dissertation to discover whether it is worth his more careful consideration, and pausing to gather the argument of a page in a few swift glances...The medieval reader, with few exceptions, did not read as we; he was in the stage of our muttering childhood learner; each word for him a separate entity and at times a problem, which he whispered to himself when he found the solution." (p.10)

Writing enabled lengthy and detailed descriptions to be made and the advent of printing significantly increased the importance of exactitude over manuscript description. Printing was the first mass production technology and books share the essential characteristic of any mass-produced item — uniformity. A printed book looks exactly the same and contains exactly the same content as any other book in the same edition. This was never true of any two manuscripts, even if they were produced by the same scribe. Errors were common and unlikely to be detected by readers who rarely had an opportunity to compare multiple copies of the same manuscript. This problem was most acute with illustrations which were subject to continuous corruption as they were repeatedly copied by successive scribes.

---

8   The significance in the above claim is in the final assertion rather than the validity of the three inventions since previous lists of 'critical' inventions have included the stirrup, the mechanical clock, silk, distilling, the magnetic compass, double-entry bookkeeping, spectacles, the insurance contract, universities and even the long hose and beret!

The introduction of printing changed the form of books as well as the way in which their content was regarded. Printing was associated with commercial publishing, and although the first printed books were exact copies of manuscripts this fidelity was soon replaced by a commitment to technical improvement in order to gain a competitive advantage. Well before the year 1500, printers had started to experiment with different typefaces, running heads, footnotes, tables of contents, figures and cross references. For example, Peter Schöffer — Gutenberg's partner — printed a prospectus for his firm's books which described them as being more readable, having more complete and better arranged indexes and as having received more careful proof reading and better editing.[9]

As library and publishers' catalogues grew larger, new methods of cataloguing became essential. The eighth century library at York had a rhymed book list and other catalogues were equally idiosyncratic. Although a standard alphabetic order was employed in the Greek library at Alexandria, the convention was used infrequently and somewhat unsystematically through the period of manuscript culture. Only with the advent of printing did it become general practice.

The adoption of a standard alphabetic ordering was an important aid in transferring the book from a repository of utterances for verbal recitation to a visual object for critical examination. Alphabetic ordering, along with Arabic page numbering,[10] revolutionised indexing. In the era of papyrus scrolls and manuscripts, making a reference to a specific sentence or section was virtually impossible. While scrolls often had line numbers, they originated as a metric for the payment of scribes rather than for purposes of reference. Similarly with manuscripts, indexing was often not worth the effort since no two manuscripts were ever exactly the same in terms of page numbers or even content. According to Witty (1965), manuscripts with even basic alphabetic indexing appeared no earlier than the 14th century and this often involved ordering only to the level of the first syllable. Indexes often consisted of sentences drawn from the text ordered alphabetically according to a "catchword" as in a contemporary key-word-in-context (KWIC) index. Page numbering is another feature that is taken for granted today but only appeared after printing. The numbers were originally placed on each leaf rather than on each page and were used to help the binder get the leaves in the correct order.

As printing reduced the need to maximise page filling for reasons of economy, so the number of contractions/abbreviations reduced and the amount of white space

---

9 Could this have been the first claim for a user-friendly design?

10 See Dantzig (1954) for a full account of the impact of the introduction of Arabic numerals and the concept of zero on science and mathematics.

increased, thus allowing greater separation of words, sentences and the visual separation of paragraphs.

The term 'index' also reveals the influence of oral/rhetorical tradition on manuscripts since it was a shortened form of 'index locorum' or 'index locorum communium'. These were the index of places or index of common places (mental images) where various arguments could be retrieved from memory. This alteration of practical meaning of the term illustrates the shift from verbal to visual orientation that accompanied printing. A second example is the use of figures. Accurate drawings were included in very early 'original' texts (e.g., Galen's text on medicine) but were frequently omitted, for reasons of economy, when the works were copied. If they were copied, their value quickly diminished:

"Hand done technical drawings...soon deteriorated in manuscripts because even skilled artists miss the point of an illustration they are copying unless they are supervised by an expert in the the field the illustrations refer to. Otherwise, a sprig of white clover copied by a succession of artists unfamiliar with real white clover can end up looking like asparagus." (Ong, 1982, p.126)

While printed illustrations, by way of woodcuts and subsequently more accurate engravings, were initially employed by printers with little apparent care (incorrect captioning, reversed images and the frequent use of a very limited range of images), their introduction assisted in the development of technical texts. Indeed, it is possible to argue that the introduction of accurately printed figures, the new concern with accurate description and the increased circulation of texts enabled modern science to develop in the 16th century. Similarly, Eisenstein (1979) has discussed the the impact of the increased visual order given to books through printing:

"The systematic arrangement of titles; the tables which followed strict alphabetical order; the indexes and cross-references to accurately numbered paragraphs all show how new tools available to printers helped to bring more order and method into a significant body of public law." (p.105)

She goes on to argue, like Ong, that the order imposed on printed words was internalised and led to more systematic approaches to information in general:

"Increasing familiarity with regularly numbered pages, punctuation marks, section breaks, running heads, indices, and so forth, helped to reorder the thought of *all* readers, whatever their profession or craft." (p.105)

This increasing bias towards visualization of knowledge can be seen in the dialectical approach to organizing knowledge favoured by Pierre de la Ramee (Petrus Ramus) in the 16th century. Ramus was an influential and, even by the standards of his time, highly controversial[11] French academic who firmly believed that the teaching and learning of any discipline could be greatly improved through the application of systematic structuring. Ramus was a confirmed humanist and rejected the artificial memory techniques which, although originating in classical Greek and Roman times, were associated with both medieval monastic scholasticism and the occult. According to Yeates (1966):

> "...one of the chief aims of the Ramist movement for the reform and simplification of education was to provide a new and better way of memorising all subjects. This was to be done by a new method whereby every subject was to be arranged in 'dialectical order'. This order was set out in schematic form in which the 'general' or inclusive aspects of the subject came first, descending thence through a series of dichotomised classifications to the 'specials' or individual aspects. Once a subject was set out in its dialectical order it was memorised in this order from the schematic presentation — the famous Ramist epitome." (p.232)

For Ramus, the dialectical analysis of subject matter by way of a hierarchical class system is optimal because dialectical order is 'natural' to the mind. This approach can be clearly seen to be another memory system but one which is based on memorising a visual schematic representation. Ong has claimed that Ramus' perspective was a consequence of the increased tendency for visual ordering fostered by the arrival of printing. However, it is possible to find evidence within manuscript culture of visual categorisation in two dimensional space — e.g., the manuscripts employing the 'scholastic method' described by Evans (1980).

Although his work was incredibly popular and influential at the time among the protestant merchantile classes, it never achieved academic respectability and can be seen as something of a dead end. A possible reason for this is suggested by Figure 5 which shows the life of Cicero according to Ramus. The main events in Cicero's life are presented as a hierarchical tree. While the graphical presentation may have aided memorisation, the end hardly justifies the means. The first dichotomy contrasts his life and death and many of the lower order items are similarly vacuous. A major motivation for Ramus' work was the need for memorisation as a cornerstone of education but this requirement became less important with the arrival of print culture and the school text book.

---

11   His M.A. was entitled "Whatever Aristotle has said is a fabrication."

The Life of Cicero

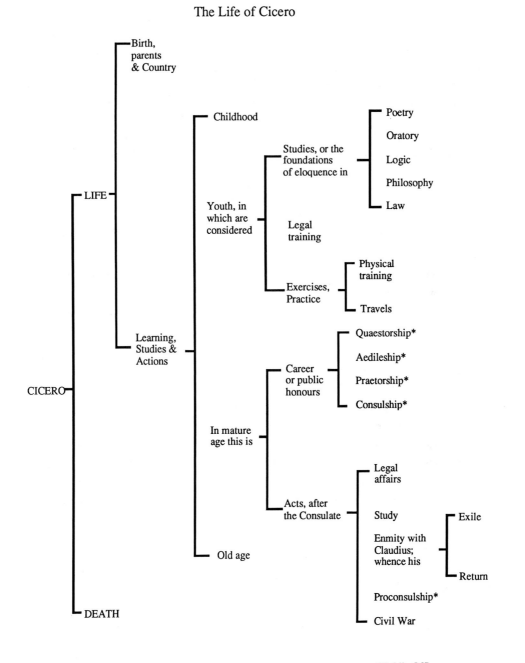

Figure 5: The life of Cicero according to Ramus, 1576.

The implications for hypertext

We have seen how technological advances in modes of representation (i.e., from oral to literate transmission) can change not only what is said but can also shape the mental processes which generate the thoughts themselves. This sounds similar to the claims expressed at the very beginning of the chapter, i.e., that widespread hypertext representation may herald an era of pluralistic rather than linear thought. However, while hypertext might seem to represent a radical change in medium, it is not likely to result in a revolution in thought; it is a comparatively trivial change compared to the advent of popular literacy.

Although hypertext differs significantly from printed text in its 'arbitrary' structure, it shares many similarities for the reader. Hypertexts, despite their node and link structure, are still composed of units of text and there is no reason to believe that, at the paragraph level at least, these are read any differently from units of conventional paper or other electronic text. At a higher level of organisation, it is common for the reader of a hypertext to be frequently presented with alternative routes through the text. However, although the reader may be encouraged to make more active choices, this still results in a 'serial' route through the text since only one node can be accessed at a time.

This is not to say that popular use of hypertext will result in an unchanged conception of 'text' but that the changes might not be obvious ones. An appropriate parallel might be with the changes in attitude that accompanied the introduction and usage of printed texts. Although the first books (incunabula) were printed versions of manuscripts and therefore were largely the same in terms of content, the fact that they were printed rather than hand-written resulted in significant conceptual changes. Uniformity, order and repeatability are characteristic qualities of the printing process but they were soon characteristic of the way that knowledge was organized — soon after the introduction of printing there was an significant increase in alphabetical ordering, indexing, bibliographies and classificatory systems in a variety of disciplines.

What changes are likely to be associated with popular use of hypertext? Almost any suggestion is likely to be highly speculative at such an early stage, but by way of example consider the issue of textual authority. A printed text has always had an authoritative quality that is not granted to a speech — in general, people are more likely to believe what they read than what they hear, especially when the text is couched in official terms and printed in an appropriate style. In a similar way, almost irrespective of the content, a perfectly reproduced typeset document has an authority that is simply not available to a manuscript. The reasons for this are varied and largely historical and include: the rôle of the Bible as the prototypical book; the very long period when literacy was skill restricted to the educated elite and a period nearly as long when individuals learned to read (often the Bible) but not write; finally there is the restricted access to publishing imposed by financial considerations. At the level of the individual text the physical presence of the document confirms the enduring quality of writing over the ephemeral nature of speech and reinforces the separate identity of a specific text. This aspect has long been recognised by the publishing industry which has developed a variety of ways of adding authority to texts by selective use of impressive bindings, decoration, typography and weight of paper.

In complete contrast, an electronic text is strikingly neutral. It has little physical presence and its shape is fluid rather than fixed. The author or editor (and increasingly they are the same person) experiences the generation of an electronic text as an endless round of amendments, some major but the majority minor. The creation of a printed book traditionally consisted of a series of discrete drafts since the text soon becomes unreadable after a certain number of editorial comments have been written on the typescript.[12] This contrast is maintained after the publishing date since the cost of re-setting a printed book ensures that revised versions are kept to a minimum; there is little cost associated with changing an electronic text.

The contrast is even stronger for the reader who experiences a printed text in much the same way on every occasion while the electronic text is constantly changing before his eyes — this impression is strongest with scrolling displays but is still true of paged displays unless the screen refresh is almost instantaneous. In addition, every text displayed on a given display system is likely to look the same since a common font (or restricted range of fonts) will probably be used for all. Hypertext compounds this weakening by allowing readers to either jump from text to text with ease or by presenting texts which are composed largely of inclusions from other documents. Whether these differences are strong enough to reduce the reader's willingness to question the authority of the text remains open to empirical evaluation but there seem *a priori* grounds to believe that it could well be true.

Turning to the second theme of the chapter, we have seen how the fixed physical form of the printed text, far from still being a constraint, has largely been transcended. The skills that we have acquired for text handling in the broadest sense make serial reading a rare strategy outside of fiction. Our current experience with (reading and writing) text reflects two complimentary, organizing influences. The detached, linear mode of thought that results from alphabetic literacy and the

---

[12] This distinction is less true now since printed texts are increasingly being created on word processors rather than typewriters.

text handling skills that develop with continuous interaction with sophisticated printed materials. These skills allow rapid silent reading, skim reading, reading tables and graphs and intensive use of indices and contents lists. The skills, enabled by the years spent in education, the profusion of printed material, the standardisation of print formats and the evolution of typography, have allowed us to overcome many of the supposed limitations of the written record.

Judging by the current generation of hypertext system interfaces, it would appear that the majority of designers are unaware of these developments and skills. Instead of attempting to provide information-rich screens which have been designed with due regard to typography and graphical layout, all too often the user is presented with comparatively little textual, and even less contextual, information and a number of choices concerning additional screens of information. In order to gain an informed impression of the hypertext's coverage in terms of breadth and depth, it is therefore necessary to scan a considerable number of screens.

By way of example, consider a broadsheet newspaper like *The Times* which has achieved a presentation format that maximises information display with rapid access for the user. A quick scan of the complete paper can be completed in minutes. In contrast, to display the contents of a single page of this newspaper on a standard (24 line x 80 character) microcomputer screen would require 25 separate screens — to display the whole newspaper would require in the order of a 1000 screens. Even if the hypertext was displayed on a larger workstation screen, browsing would still represent a considerable task. Yet hypertext is frequently suggested as a way by which readers can browse[13] large databases rather than employ structured search strategies.

Despite these current weaknesses, hypertext's true potential surely lies in its ability to improve access to the growing corpus of electronic information. Current on-line databases hold enormous quantities of information but their interfaces are frequently too daunting for the untrained or casual user. They may well hold the information required but they frequently require a trained intermediary to select the appropriate database and formulate an appropriate search query. 'Trawling' with fuzzily defined targets is definitely not recommended. Hypertext could provide a supportive interface to these, and future, databases (cf. Marchionini and Shneiderman, 1988).

However, hypertext could be much more than a superior access mechanism for today's text-based databases. In a multimedia guise within a teaching/learning context, it offers much better ways of presenting information compared to

---

13 This is just one type of browsing — open-ended browsing with no specific targets. Other types of browsing, e.g., following a particular idea or theme, may well be better supported by hypertext.

traditional printed texts. Consider the advantages of being able to build multimedia hypertexts for schools and students which include video and sound as well as text and graphics — as described in Chapter 1. Obvious applications include natural sciences, art, drama, music and social history but the possibilities are really only limited by the imagination.

Such applications may significantly improve the quality of our teaching/learning tools, hopefully resulting in increased breadth, complexity and integration of teaching and learning, but it is not clear how 'immersion' in hypertext will affect the way that we mentally structure our world. Linear argumentation is more a consequence of alphabetic writing than of printed books and it remains to be seen if hypertext presentation will significantly erode this predominant convention for mentally ordering our world.

CHAPTER THREE

USERS, TASKS AND INFORMATION

"A man ought to read just as inclination leads him; for what he reads as a task will do him little good."

Boswell's Life of Johnson

Introduction

In Chapter 1 we said that when talking about hypertext we are referring to *people* using *information* to perform some *task*. These concepts will be discussed further here as we look at some attributes of the user, information and task that can guide us in the design and rôle of usable hypertext applications. The complexity of issues involved and the range of applications and tasks that hypertext may be used for imply that we cannot talk of hypertext as a unified form of presentation any more than we can meaningfully describe a typical text. It is important to understand from the outset therefore that when discussing hypertext we do not seek simplistic answers to questions such as "Is hypertext better than paper?" or "Do people learn more from hypertext systems than standard texts?"

Users are people. They have skills, habits, motivations, intelligence, intentions and a whole host of other attributes that they bring to the computer when using hypertext. Modern cognitive psychology and ergonomics have accumulated a substantial amount of information about humans using computers. It is not the intention of this chapter to review this work (a useful non-specialist introduction can be found in Shneiderman, 1987a) but rather to introduce readers to its basic orientation so that they might better understand the relevance to hypertext.

The rapid development of information technology over the last decade or so means that to some extent we are all users (even if we are unaware of it), and contemporary thinking rightly stresses that technology should be designed with users' needs in mind. In the hypertext domain it is likely that potential users will

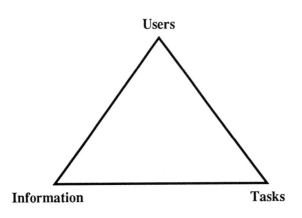

Figure 6: The important interaction variables for hypertext.

come from all walks of life and age groups. Hypertext applications will not exist only in libraries, schools or offices but will also be found in museums (e.g., HyperTIES), tourist information centres (e.g., Glasgow On-line) and eventually, in the home. Thus when we talk of hypertext and its uses, it is important that we try to place our discussion in a specific context by looking at the first element of our triumvirate and asking 'who are the target users?'

The information that users deal with when interacting with contemporary computer systems varies tremendously. With hypertext such variation is equally apparent. Hypertext systems can be used to manipulate and present lengthy texts such as journal articles (McKnight, Richardson and Dillon, 1990), encyclopædias (Shneiderman, 1987b), computer programs (Monk *et al.*, 1988) or English literature (Landow, 1990) to name but a few current applications. In fact, there is no reason why any information could not be presented in hypertext form — rather, the question is, looking at the second element of our triumvirate, 'what sort of information would benefit from such presentation?'

Just as users and information vary, so too do the tasks that can be performed on computers. Software is (or should be) designed with specific tasks in mind which it will support, e.g., desk-top publishing, database management, process control, statistical analysis and so forth. Equally with hypertext, users will perform a variety of tasks — the third part of the triumvirate — and consequently hypermedia must be designed accordingly. In short, when we consider users, information and tasks we draw the conclusion that different implementations of the hypertext concept will be required in different domains.

It makes little sense to talk about users, information and tasks as if they were independent entities because clearly they are not. By definition, a user must be using something, i.e., performing a task, the very act of which implies information transfer. Therefore, a convenient trichotomisation is not possible. This chapter will attempt to describe the relevant issues relating to each of these elements before demonstrating how our understanding of all three is important to hypermedia.

The user as reader

Invariably, the user of a hypertext application will be reading material from a visual display unit (though authoring is increasingly possible and will be discussed in detail in Chapter 5). Thus, it is worth considering what we know about reading and its relevance to screen-displayed text. Reading is one of the most intensively studied cognitive activities, with serious investigation of it as a psychological phenomenon commencing in the last century (for a review of work at that time see Huey, 1908). Since then, researchers have analysed the processes involved in reading, from the level of eye-movements across the page to that of how readers comprehend visually presented material. It is not the intention of this chapter to summarise such work or present sections of it in great detail (a comprehensive review can be found in Beech and Colley, 1987). However a brief description of the salient aspects is relevant to the present discussion.

The psychology of reading

When reading, light enters the eye through the cornea, passes via the aqueous humour to an opening in the iris known as the pupil where it is focused by the lens. From here it passes through the vitreous humour to the innervated portion of the eye called the retina (see Figure 7). From the retina the light signal passes down the optic nerve to the brain. The retina is effectively split down the middle and light signals impinging on the outer side of the retina go to the same outer side of the brain, but those from the nasal side cross at the optic chiasma, just behind the eyes, and go to opposite sides of the brain. This is obviously a gross simplification of the processes involved but serves to highlight the complexity of the transformation of light into image.

As you read the words on this page, your eye movements may feel smooth but actually consist of a series of rapid jumps and rests, termed 'saccades' and 'fixations' respectively. Saccades last approximately 25-30 milliseconds, fixations 200-250 milliseconds, so the eyes are stationary[1] for about 90% of the reading time. Readers of English normally proceed from left to right, one line at a time,

---

[1] The term 'stationary' is in fact a misnomer as the eyes are always oscillating slightly. Such imperceptible movements are necessary to avoid image loss as a result of a stabilised retinal image inducing cell adaptation in the eye.

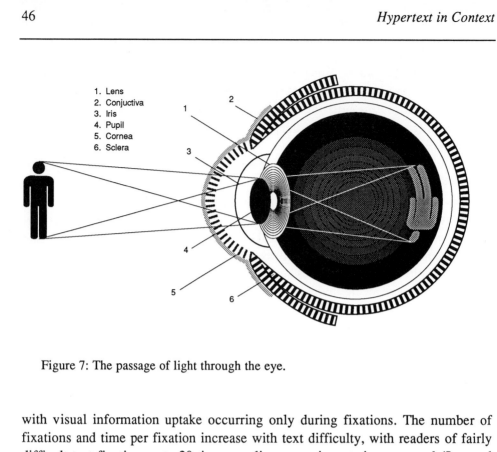

1. Lens
2. Conjuctiva
3. Iris
4. Pupil
5. Cornea
6. Sclera

Figure 7: The passage of light through the eye.

with visual information uptake occurring only during fixations. The number of fixations and time per fixation increase with text difficulty, with readers of fairly difficult text fixating up to 20 times per line, sometimes twice per word (Just and Carpenter, 1980). As this implies, regressions (i.e., backward movements of the eyes to review already fixated text) occur also. Readers can process a maximum of 10 characters either side of a fixation point, i.e., 20 characters at the most (McConkie and Rayner, 1975). This is known as their perceptual span and in readers of English is biased to the right of their fixation point.[2]

While there is some agreement about the processes involved at this level, theoretical differences emerge when we come to describe letter and word recognition. It is clear that both letter and word recognition processes occur, perhaps interactively, on the basis of features such as shape, size, form and context, although the relative importance attributed to any one of these factors varies. There has been some success in modelling these processes on computers (see, for example, McClelland and Rumelhart, 1981) but a complete theoretical explanation that accounts for all the empirical observations on these phenomena has yet to be presented.

---

[2] This bias is a reflection of how a language is laid out in written form. In readers of Hebrew, for example, the bias is to the left reflecting the fact that Hebrew is written from right to left.

The situation is even less clear at the level of comprehension, i.e., how do people form an understanding of what they read? It seems obvious that readers draw inferences from particular sentences and form representations at different levels of what is happening in the text. Various models of comprehension have been proposed to explain this. Thorndyke (1977) proposed a set of 'grammar rules' by which the reader forms a structure in their mind of how the story fits together. Van Dijk and Kintsch (1983) proposed a very detailed model involving an analysis of the propositions of a text, leading to the development of a 'macropropositional hierarchy' influenced by the reader's model of the situation represented in the text. More recently, Johnson-Laird (1983) and Garnham (1986) have proposed a 'mental models' approach to text comprehension that involves the reader representing the meaning of the text as an imaginary, updatable model in their mind.

In view of the lack of agreement on the nature of comprehension, it is not surprising that measuring comprehension has also proved problematic. It might seem a simple enough matter to ask readers a number of questions about the text they have just read, but it is difficult to know whether memory for detail is being tested rather then comprehension. Furthermore, texts may be open to interpretation, the richness of which depends on the reader's contextual knowledge and appreciation of the author's message — all factors which make comprehension measurement a complicated issue.

It is also clear that readers acquire knowledge of how texts are structured or organised and can use these structural models to predict the likely meaning of the text (van Dijk and Kintsch, 1983) or the location of information within it. Furthermore, readers have been shown to remember spatial location of information within a text after reading it (Rothkopf, 1971). These are findings pertinent to the development of hypertext applications and will be discussed in greater detail in Chapter 4.

Thus, the psychological study of reading shows us the complexity of the processes performed when reading even simple material such as isolated words and sentences. It is also clear that on matters such as comprehension, psychology has invested heavily in theoretical constructs which attempt to account for mental representation of the text but do not necessarily provide us with useful methods for assessing readers' understanding of the material.[3] These issues have relevance to the development and use of hypertext systems and will be raised in several guises throughout this book, especially when we talk about usability or applications of the technology in specific domains such as education. In the following section we

---

[3]   van Dijk and Kintsch's model is exceptional in that it doubles as a method for assessing comprehension by analysing readers' written summaries of material. The extent to which this method is useful with lengthy texts is debatable however.

discuss the potential differences between reading from paper and screen. The psychological view of reading offers an explanatory framework within which some of the findings in this area can be interpreted.

Reading from screens

Not surprisingly, a good deal of research has addressed the potential difference between reading material from paper and reading from screen. A recent review by Dillon *et al.* (1988) highlighted five potential differences between the media:

- Speed
- Accuracy
- Fatigue
- Comprehension
- Preference

In general, people read 20–30% slower from typical screens, where 'typical' is taken to mean a low-resolution 24-line display with white (or green) text on a black background (Muter *et al.*, 1982; Wright and Lickorish, 1983; Gould and Grischkowsky, 1984). However, the emphasis in hypertext on easy selectability of links, multiple windows and so forth has meant that such packages are implemented on systems with large, high-resolution screens with black characters on a white background. Under such conditions (with the addition of anti-aliased characters) Gould *et al.* (1987) reported no significant difference in reading speed between screen and paper. The explanation for this probably lies at the image quality level: the human eye is better able to perceive and distinguish rapidly between letters and words presented on paper than they are with more typical screens; as technology improves and screen quality approaches that of paper, reading speed differences may cease to be an issue for the hypertext user.

'Accuracy' of reading usually refers to performance in some form of proof-reading task, although there is debate in the literature about what constitutes a valid task. Typically, the number of errors located in an experimental text has been used as a measure (Wright and Lickorish, 1983; Gould and Grischkowsky, 1984). While it is probably true to say that few users of hypertext will be performing such routine spelling checks, many more users are likely to be searching for specific information, scanning a section of text and so forth. For the more visually or cognitively demanding tasks such as these, a performance deficit for screen-based presentation is more likely (Creed *et al.*, 1987; Wilkinson and Robinshaw, 1987). In a study by the present authors (McKnight, Dillon and Richardson, 1990), subjects were asked to locate answers to a set of questions in a text using either a paper version, a word processor document or one of two hypertext versions.

Results showed an accuracy effect favouring paper and the linear-format word processor version, suggesting a structural familiarity effect. Obviously, more experimental work comparing hypertext and paper on a range of texts and tasks is needed.

With both speed and accuracy, a performance deficit may not be immediately apparent to the user. However, the same cannot usually be said of fatigue effects. There is a popular belief that reading from screens leads to greater fatigue, so will hypertext have users reaching for the Optrex? Gould and Grischkowsky (1984) obtained responses to a 16-item "Feelings Questionnaire" which required subjects to rate their fatigue, levels of tension, mental stress and so forth after several work periods on a computer and on paper. Furthermore, various visual measurements such as flicker and contrast sensitivity, visual acuity and phoria, were taken at the beginning of the day and after each work period. Neither questionnaire responses nor visual measures showed a significant effect for presentation medium. These results led the authors to conclude that good-quality VDUs in themselves do not produce fatiguing effects, although the findings have been disputed by Wilkinson and Robinshaw (1987). Nevertheless, to suggest as these latter authors do that Gould's equipment was 'too good to show an effect' throws us back on the definition of a 'typical' screen. Since typical for the hypertext user is likely to be of better quality than the average microcomputer screen, it suggests that visual fatigue may be no more of a problem than for a draughtsman facing a piece of white paper illuminated by fluorescent light.

The effect of presentation medium on comprehension is particularly difficult to assess because of the lack of agreement about how comprehension can best be measured. If the validity of such methods as post-task questions or standardised reading tests is accepted, it appears that comprehension is not affected by presentation medium (see, for example, Kak, 1981). However, such results typically involve the use of an 'electronic copy' of a single paper document. The hypertext context differs significantly in terms of both document structure and size. A hypertext document is freed from the traditional structure of printed documents and is also likely to be just one member of an inter-related library. The issue of comprehension takes on a new dimension in this context.

It is widely argued that with hypertext, the departure from linear structure makes it difficult for the user to build a 'mental model' of the text and increases the potential for 'getting lost' (although the extent to which this is also true for complex and extensive paper document systems remains unanswered). We will address issues of navigation and readers' models in more detail in Chapter 4, but for the present it appears that the cognitive and manipulative demands of hypertext *could* lead to a comprehension deficit. If there is no time pressure on the user, this deficit may simply appear as a speed deficit — the user takes longer to achieve the same level of comprehension. However, if time pressure is involved a comprehension deficit is more likely to be observed. This may have particular relevance to educational applications.

No matter what the experimental findings are, a user's *preference* is likely to be a determining feature in the success or failure of any technology. Several studies have reported a preference for paper over screen (e.g., Cakir *et al.*, 1980), although some of these may now be discounted on the grounds that they date from a time when screen technology was far below current standards. Experience is likely to play a large rôle, but users who dislike technology are unlikely to gain sufficient experience to alter their attitude. Therefore the onus is on developers to design good hypertext systems using high quality screens to overcome such users' reticence. What seems to have been overlooked as far as formal investigation is concerned is the natural flexibility of books and paper over VDUs; books are portable, cheap, apparently "natural" in our culture, personal and easy to use. The extent to which such "common-sense" variables influence user preferences is not yet well-understood.

Conclusion

To date, the work on reading from screens is useful in highlighting the likely problems that may be encountered by readers using hypertext. However, it must be noted that much of this work was carried out on poorer quality screens than are currently available on many hypertext systems. Furthermore, studies have tended to employ tasks that bear little resemblance to the type of activities which hypertext users perform. As technology improves, any differences resulting purely from image quality should disappear. This still leaves the questions of accuracy, comprehension and preference open, however, and these will be considered further in the context of the text types and tasks which hypertext might be called upon to support.

Classifying information types

We live in a world where books, newspapers, comics, magazines, manuals, reports and a whole host of other document forms are commonplace. We take such a range for granted, yet there are significant differences between these documents in terms of content, style, format, literary merit, usefulness, size and so forth. As with tasks, it is certain that hypertext will have more impact on certain types of document than others and will almost certainly create new document forms that are not feasible with paper. Hence it would be useful to develop a framework that would facilitate the classification of texts.

At first glance, it might appear that such a classification would be relatively easy to develop. Obvious distinctions can be drawn between fiction and non-fiction, technical and non-technical, serious and humorous, paperback and hardback and so forth, which discriminate between texts in a relatively unambiguous manner. However, such discriminations are not necessarily informative in terms of how the text is used or the readers' views of the contents — aspects which should be apparent from any typology aiming to distinguish meaningfully between texts.

The categorisation of texts has received some attention from linguists and typographers (see Waller, 1987, for an excellent review). For example, de Beaugrande (1980) defines a text type as:

> "a distinctive configuration of relational dominances obtaining between or among elements of the surface text, the textual world, stored knowledge patterns and a situation of occurrence" (p.197)

and offers the following illustrations: descriptive, narrative, argumentative, literary, poetic, scientific, didactic and conversational. However, de Beaugrande freely admits that these categories are not mutually exclusive and are not distinguishable on any one dimension. Waller adds that it is not at all clear where texts such as newspapers or advertisements fit in such a typology, and proposes instead an analysis of text types in terms of three kinds of underlying structure:

- topic structure, the typographic effects which display information about the author's argument, e.g., headings
- artefact structure, the features determined by the physical nature of the document, e.g., page size
- access structure, features that serve to make the document usable, e.g., lists of contents.

In a more psychological vein, van Dijk and Kintsch (1983) use the term "discourse types" to describe the macrostructural regularities present in real-world texts such as crime stories or psychological research reports. According to their theory of discourse comprehension, such types facilitate readers' predictions about the likely episodes or events in a text and thus support accurate macroproposition formation. In other words, the reader can utilise this awareness of the text's typical form or contents to aid comprehension of the material. In their view, such types are the literary equivalent of scripts or frames[4] and play an important rôle in their

---

4   A script (or frame) is an organised knowledge structure derived from the extraction of common elements of a range of situations. The most common example in the psychological literature is the restaurant script.

model of discourse comprehension. However, they stop short of providing a classification or typology themselves and it is not clear how this work can be extended to inform the design of hypertext documents.

From a less theoretical standpoint Wright (1980) describes texts in terms of their application domains:

- domestic (e.g., instructions for using appliances)
- functional (e.g., work-related manuals)
- advanced literacy (e.g., magazines or novels)

She uses these categories to emphasise the range of texts that exist and to highlight the fact that reading research must become aware of this tremendous diversity. Research into the presentation and reading of one text may have little or no relevance to, and may even require separate theoretical and methodological standpoints from, other texts.

It is doubtful if any one classification or typology can adequately cope with the range of paper information sources that abound in the real world. In Wright's (1980) categorisation, for example, the distinction between functional and domestic blurs considerably when one thinks of the number of electronic gadgets now found in the home which have associated operational and trouble-shooting manuals (not least the home computer). This is not a criticism of any one classification but rather an indication that each has a limit to its range of applicability, outside of which it ceases to have relevance. Thus, one can find situations in which any typology fails to distinguish clearly between texts. We should not necessarily expect classifications designed for typographers to help developers of hypertext systems.

Some classifications aimed specifically at the hypertext domain are beginning to emerge. Wright and Lickorish (1989) for example, distinguishes between texts in terms of their information structure and uses this to guide the design of hypertext versions. In particular, they highlight linear, modular, hierarchic and matrix document structures and argue convincingly that such structures have implications for the type of linkages, visual appearance and navigation support that need to be provided by authors. Thus, the navigation support necessary for a linear structure (such as a set of instructions) might be a series of loops initiated by the reader through pointing, while readers of modular texts (such as an encyclopædia) will require more explicit information about where they came from and where they currently are in the information space, since looping will not be as common with such texts.

An alternative approach to text classification by Dillon and McKnight (1990) involved using a technique known as repertory grid analysis to describe readers' views of texts. Rather than devising a formal classification, this work resulted in a

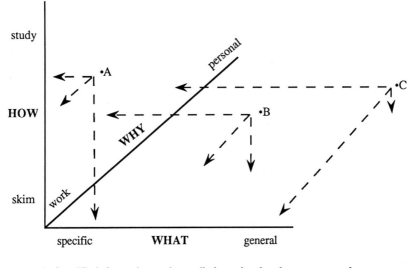

A: Specific information, to be studied, work-related text, e.g., a relevant scientific article.
B: Less specific than A, can be read quickly, general work-related text, e.g., technical magazine.
C: Non-technical, can be skim read, personal interest, e.g., newspaper.

Figure 8: A three-way classification of texts based on How, Why and What attributes.

framework for considering text types. They concluded that readers conceive of text in terms of three characteristics: *how* they are read, *why* they are read and *what* sort of information they contain. By viewing text types according to these attributes, it is easy to distinguish between, say, a novel and a journal. The former is likely to be read serially (*how*), for leisure (*why*) and contain general or non-technical information (*what*), whereas the latter is more likely to be studied or read more than once (*how*), for professional reasons (*why*) and contain technical information which includes graphics (*what*). This approach can be represented in terms of a three-dimensional 'classification space' as shown in Figure 8. Here, three texts are distinguished according to their positions relative to the *How*, *Why* and *What* axes The descriptors study–skim, work–personal and general–specific may vary and are only intended as examples. Different people may employ very different terms. However, the authors argue that they are still likely to be descriptors that pertain to the attributes *How*, *Why* and *What*.

According to this perspective any particular text may be classified in several ways depending on the reader and their information needs. Not only does this mean that a text may be seen differently by two readers but also that a reader may view a text differently according to their needs at any one time. The hypertext version should thus be designed with these principles in mind, analysing the *how*, *why* and *what* questions in detail before attempting to build an electronic version of a text. The authors use the example of a novel and suggest that, from a classification of this text type in terms of these three aspects, we would not expect a hypertext version to have much potential. However, if we consider the full range of *how* and *why* attributes that emerge as a result of analysing novels, one can envisage an educational context where various parts of the text are analysed and compared linguistically, thereby rendering a suitable hypertext version more useful than paper. In other words, a hypertext novel may not be suitable for reading on the train but it may be ideal for the student of English literature.

Conclusion

The classifications of information types that have been proposed are based on numerous criteria: underlying, typographic and macro structures, application domain, readers' perceptions and attributes of use. No doubt other classifications will emerge, perhaps based on altogether different criteria than any described here. Structural distinctions are likely to remain important as hypertext creates new document types based on innovative electronic structures, but distinctions based on usage patterns and readers' views will always be relevant. It is unlikely that any one classification scheme is best or suitable for all situations.

Reading as an information manipulation task

By 'task', we usually mean the performance of any goal-directed activity. In the context of reading, the term includes identifying, locating and processing relevant material. With texts this may involve looking for a book title and shelf number in a library catalogue, reading a novel, browsing a newspaper, proof-reading a legal contract or studying a mathematical theorem. In fact, if we define reading as the visual-to-cognitive processing of textual and graphical material in an information-seeking manner, and extend its traditional boundaries to include the procedures that necessarily precede contact between eye and source such as scanning bookshelves or selecting a correct edition of a journal (i.e., gaining access to the material), then we begin to get some idea of the diversity of tasks that are performed by readers.[5]

At present, hypertext systems have only scratched the surface of the range of

---

[5]   Even in the comparatively narrow domain of experimental psychology, variations in the definition of reading exist. See for example Just and Carpenter's (1980) model of reading which includes comprehension of the material and Crowder's (1982) definition which explicitly excludes it.

tasks they will eventually support. Indeed, hypertext applications may well eventually give rise to tasks that have not been thought of or cannot yet be effectively performed. Whatever the final outcome, it is clear that they have the potential to play a significant rôle in many reading scenarios.

The diversity of reading tasks

It is worth considering how people use the paper medium to perform information manipulation tasks if we want to understand how hypermedia may not only support them but offer advantages to the user. Laboratory studies of reading have tended, in the main, to concentrate on a very limited subset of tasks such as locating spelling errors on pages of text (Gould *et al.*, 1987), making sense of anaphoric references in sentences (Clark, 1977) or recalling episodes in short stories (Thorndyke, 1977). Although some of this work has been invaluable in advancing our knowledge of the reader, it tells us very little about information usage in the real world or how to design hypertext systems for people.

People do not all interact with texts in the same fashion, and although texts may appear linear, this rarely ensures a serial style of reading. Furthermore, the same text may be read in different ways depending on the reader's task. This much is intuitively obvious from self-observation. Consider the differences between reading a newspaper and novel. The former is likely to consist of a mixture of scanning and browsing in an unplanned fashion, reacting to interesting headlines or pictures, while the latter is more likely to involve serial reading of the complete text. Next, consider the differences between reading an interesting article in the newspaper and checking on a sports result or looking for the TV page. The former will involve the so-called higher-level cognitive functions of comprehension while the latter will be more of a recognition task. It is clear that while all these scenarios can be described as reading, they vary widely in terms of how and why the reader interacts with the text as well as the text type under consideration. Characterising these differences would be useful for hypertext developers because it would suggest ways in which hypertext documents should be developed in order to optimise reading performance.

Researchers as early as Huey (1908) were aware of the diversity of tasks typically performed by readers, and to this day it has remained generally accepted that this variety is worthy of consideration. For example, on the subject of electronic journals Wright (1987) drew attention to the fact that, depending on what information is being sought, readers may employ browsing, skimming, studying, cross-checking or linear reading. However, while it is possible to compile lists of likely reading tasks and their performance characteristics, it is entirely another matter to validate them empirically.

Observing task performance

Schumacher and Waller (1985) make the point that reading research has tended to concentrate on outcome measures (such as speed or comprehension) rather than process ones (what the reader does with the text). Without doubt, the main obstacle to obtaining accurate process data is devising a suitable, non-intrusive observation method. While numerous techniques for measuring eye-movements during reading now exist, it is not at all clear from eye-movement records what the reader was thinking or trying to do at any particular time. Furthermore, use of such equipment is rarely non-intrusive, often requiring the reader to remain immobile through the use of head restraints, bite bars and so forth, or read the text one line at a time from a computer display — hardly equatable to normal reading conditions!

Less intrusive methods such as the use of light pens in darkened environments to highlight the portion of the text currently viewed (Whalley and Fleming, 1975), or modified reading stands with semi-silvered glass which reflect the readers eye movements in terms of current text position to a video camera (Pugh, 1979), are examples of the lengths to which researchers have gone in order to record reading behaviour. However, none of these are ideal as they alter the reading environment, sometimes drastically, and only their staunchest advocate would describe them as non-intrusive.

Verbal protocols of people interacting with texts — asking them to 'think aloud' — require no elaborate equipment and can be elicited wherever a subject normally reads. In this way they are cheap, relatively naturalistic and physically non-intrusive. However, the techniques have been criticised for interfering with the normal processing involved in task performance (i.e., cognitive intrusion) and requiring the presence of an experimenter to sustain and record the verbal protocol (Nisbett and Wilson, 1977).

If we accept that a perfect method does not yet exist, it is important to understand the relative merits of those that are available. Eye-movement records have significantly aided theoretical developments in modelling reading (see, for example, Just and Carpenter, 1980) while use of the light-pen type of technique has demonstrated its worth in identifying the effects of various typographic cues on reading behaviour (see, for example, Schumacher and Waller, 1985). Verbal protocols have been effectively used by researchers to gain information on reading strategies (see, for example, Olshavsky, 1977). Nevertheless, such techniques have rarely been employed with the intention of assessing the likely effect of hypertext presentation on performance. More usually they have been used to test various paper document design alternatives or to shed light on reading performance in highly controlled experimental studies.

Where text is presented on computer screens it is possible to record and time the duration of displayed text, thus facilitating reasonable inference about what readers are doing.[6] However, as an attempt to analyse normal reading performance, this fails because there is no way of gauging the influence of the medium on performance, i.e., reading electronic text cannot be directly equated to reading paper. A fuller treatment of these issues can be found in Wright (1987). Nevertheless, this method provides a simple and effective way of observing gross manipulations of text without making the person aware of the recording process.

Virtually all of the work on hypertext has employed such recording techniques to monitor user navigation and use of various commands. With the advent of cheap screen recording devices it is possible to record how the entire screen display changes throughout the course of the interaction, for later replay without resorting to video recordings. While this is obviously useful, it does not solve the problem of how to assess the use of paper and its importance for hypertext design. Where paper and hypertext are directly compared, although process measures may be taken with the computer and/or video cameras, the final comparison often rests on outcome measures.

Evidence for task effects

Probably because of the difficulties outlined above, research has tended not to focus directly on how people read or the range of tasks they perform with texts. Instead, investigators normally test reading in circumstances where the task is specifically designed to manipulate experimental variables. Typically these have been: proof-reading, short story comprehension, letter or word recognition, sentence recall and so forth. In itself this is a recognition of the variable effect of task on reading. However, there have been some studies which have sought to test task effects directly. Two are described here which illustrate the range from the single sentence to the full document level.

Aaronson and Ferres (1986) had subjects read 80 sentences one word at a time from a computer screen and perform either a recall or comprehension test item after each sentence. They observed differences in the time taken to read words in a sentence depending on the task being performed. Their results supported the hypotheses that readers tend to process *structure* for retention tasks and *meaning* for comprehension tasks, i.e., their cognitions are altered according to the demands of the reading task.

Verbal protocol analyses combined with observation of readers' manipulations

---

6   In saying this we are assuming that the inferences are being drawn by a skilled evaluator with detailed knowledge of the task being performed by the reader. In the absence of these factors the recorded interaction is unlikely to yield anything worthwhile.

of text were used in a study by Dillon *et al.* (1989) to examine researchers' use of academic journals. Unlike the other studies cited, the specific intention of this work was to identify the issues that needed to be addressed in developing a hypertext database of such material.[7] The study was reasonably successful in eliciting information on individuals' style of reading, identifying their reasons for using journals and demonstrating three strategies that were typically performed: rapid scan of the contents, browsing of certain relevant sections, and full serial reading of the text. The strategies matched the tasks being performed, e.g., rapid scanning told the reader about the suitability of the article for his purposes while full serial reading was employed when the reader wanted to study the contents of the article.

Conclusion

Task demands dictate the manner in which readers manipulate information but as yet few empirically validated performance strategies have been described. A major obstacle appears to be the lack of a suitable method for measuring such behaviour. Furthermore, any task effects demonstrated with paper documents may not transfer directly to the electronic medium. Nevertheless, the sheer diversity of tasks performed with documents necessitates some consideration of the effect of task type on the manner of usage. One hypertext implementation of a document might suit some tasks but be far from optimal for others. Without appreciating the range and manner of the tasks performed with a document, the chances of designing suitable hyper-versions are reduced.

Understanding hypertext in terms of user, task and information interactions

We stated at the beginning of this chapter that questions such as "Is hypertext better than paper?" were simplistic. The previous sections on users, tasks and information should have given some indication of why we believe this is the case. In the present section some of the emerging empirical data on hypertext will be discussed in the light of the interactions between these aspects.

To date researchers and developers have, in the main, been content to discuss the apparent advantages of hypertext systems for most tasks, occasionally describing systems they have implemented and informally presenting user reactions to them (see, for example, Marchionini and Shneiderman, 1988). Such reports are difficult to assess critically and it is easy to get carried away with the hype surrounding the new medium. If one looks at the proceedings of recent conferences

---

7   The implications of this study for the design of a hypertext database are described in more detail in Chapter 7.

on hypertext (such as Hypertext '87, Hypertext II and so forth) one will find that such reports are in the majority, with well-controlled experimental papers few and far between. To be fair, it is possible that this state of affairs reflects the stage of development of these systems; they seem like a good idea and they are being developed, with formal studies being seen as appropriate only at a later stage. Nevertheless, in the absence of confirmatory data, any claims for the new medium should be treated with caution.

What data has emerged needs to be carefully considered in the light of the three elements discussed above since findings are often conflicting and any one study can only hope to answer a subset of the questions to be asked. The next section considers some of the experimental data in terms of comparisons that have been made between hypertext and paper, hypertext and linear electronic text and between various implementations of one hypertext.

Hypertext versus paper
Perhaps the most basic comparison is between hypertext and the traditional medium of paper. Given the revolutionary form of presentation afforded by hypertext this comparison is of considerable importance to both authors and readers, educators and learners.

In a widely reported study, Egan *et al.* (1989) compared students' performance on a set of tasks involving a statistics text. Students used either the standard textbook or a hypertext version displayed via SuperBook, a structured browsing system, to search for specific information in the text and write essays with the text open. Incidental learning[8] and subjective ratings were also assessed. The authors report that:

> "students using SuperBook answered more search questions correctly, wrote higher quality 'open-book' essays, and recalled certain incidental information better than students using conventional text." (p.205)

Students also significantly preferred the hypertext version to the paper text.

At first glance this is an impressive set of findings. It seems to lend firm support to the frequently expressed view that hypertext is better than paper in the educational setting (cf. Landow, 1990). However, a closer look at the experiment is revealing. For example, with respect to the search tasks, the questions posed were varied so that their wording mentioned terms contained in the body of the text, in the headings, in both of these or neither. Not surprisingly, the largest advantage to hypertext was observed where the target information was only mentioned in the

---

8   The topic of incidental learning is dealt with more fully in Chapter 6.

body of text (i.e., there were no headings referring to it). Here it is hardly surprising that the search facility of the computer out-performed humans! When the task was less biased against the paper condition, e.g., searching for information to which there are headings, no significant difference was observed. Interestingly, the poorest performance of all was for SuperBook users searching for information when the question did not contain specific references to words used anywhere in the text. In the absence of suitable search parameters or look-up terms, hypertext suddenly seemed less usable.

This is not a criticism of the study. To the authors' credit they describe their work in sufficient detail to allow one to assess this study fully. Furthermore, they freely admit that an earlier study using an identical methodology showed less difference between the media (paper even proving significantly better than hypertext for certain tasks!) Only on the basis of this were modifications made to SuperBook which led to the observations reported above.[9]

In a study by McKnight, Dillon and Richardson (1990), subjects located information in a text on the subject of wine. This was presented in one of four conditions: paper, word processor, HyperTIES or HyperCard. The tasks were designed in order to require a range of retrieval strategies on the part of the subject, i.e., while the search facility might prove useful for some questions, it could not be employed slavishly to answer all questions. This was seen as reflecting the range of activities for which such a text would be employed in the real world.

Results showed that subjects were significantly more accurate with paper than both hypertext versions though no effect for speed was observed. Subjects were also better able to estimate the document size with paper than with hypertexts and spent significantly less time in the contents and index sections of the text with the paper version. Paper and word processor versions were similar in most scores suggesting that the familiar structure inherent in both versions supported the subjects' performance.

On the face of it we have two conflicting findings on the question of paper versus hypertext. However, by appreciating the users, tasks and information types employed in these two studies we can see that they are not directly comparable in anything but a superficial manner. As evidence to support a "Yes/No" answer to the question "Is hypertext better than paper?" they are obviously limited. This is not to say that no implications can be drawn. These two experiments show that each medium has its own inherent advantages and shortcomings, e.g., hypertext is better than paper when locating specific information that is contained within the body of

---

9   This is a classic example of how testing and redesigning a system — so-called iterative user-centred design — can lead to a more usable product. If no modifications had been carried out we might have found SuperBook being cited for very different reasons!

text but seems to offer no clear advantage when readers have only an approximate idea of what they are looking for. When readers access a text for the first time on a subject for which they have no specialist knowledge and cannot formulate a precise search parameter, the familiarity of paper seems to confer certain advantages.

Hypertext versus linear electronic text

As mentioned earlier in the chapter, comparisons between paper and screen reading often favour paper because of the differences in image quality between the two media. Though hypertext systems usually run on good quality screens it is possible that image quality variables still have an influence for tasks that require fast scanning and visual detection of material. A number of studies that overcome such differences are those comparing hypertext implementations with linear, i.e., non-hypertext, electronic documents on identical screens.

Monk *et al.* (1988) report two experimental comparisons of hypertext with folding and scrolling displays for examining a computer program listing. In the first study, subjects attempted fifteen questions related to program comprehension. While no effect was observed for number of tasks answered correctly, there was a significant difference between the hypertext and scrolling browsers in terms of the rate at which tasks were performed, with hypertext proving slower. In the second study they attempted to overcome this performance deficit by providing subjects with either a map of the structure of the program or a list of section headings. The map improved performance to levels comparable with users of the scrolling browser in the first study, but the list of titles had little effect. The authors conclude that the map is a vital component of any hypertext implementation; without it too much of the user's cognitive resources are required to navigate rather than deal with the primary task.

In another study comparing hypertext with linear electronic text, Gordon *et al.* (1988) asked subjects to read two articles, one in each format. Half the subjects read general interest articles with instructions for casual reading while the rest read technical articles with instructions to learn the material. Thus it can be seen that two distinct tasks and two distinct text types were employed. Performance was assessed using post-task free recall tests and question probes, while preference was assessed using a questionnaire.

Subjects answered significantly more questions correctly with the linear format than with the hypertext and also recalled significantly more of the general interest articles in linear format. Questionnaire data revealed a general 2:1 preference for the linear format with a 3:1 ratio expressing that this format required less mental effort than hypertext. Subjects frequently stated that they were used to the linear format and found hypertext intrusive on their train of thought. Similar to the Monk *et al.* study, Gordon *et al.* conclude that navigational decisions are more difficult with the hypertext and therefore disrupt the reader, i.e., cognitive intrusion occurs. The differences between formats were greater for the general interest texts than for the technical material, suggesting possible task effects, but the authors do not discuss this in any detail. One curious aspect of this study was the use of texts on the themes "Falling in love" and "Reverse sterilization" as general interest material!

Interestingly these studies seem to suggest that the hypertext structure places an extra burden on the reader in terms of navigation and consequently leads to poorer performance. On the face of it this is not too surprising for the users and texts employed here. The subjects were familiar with the structure of the linear documents and were only constrained by the manipulation facilities available to them with the system. With the hypertext systems, though manipulation may have been faster and more direct the subjects needed not only to learn the new document structure but also suppress their existing model of where information was likely to be positioned. The fact that naïve users can perform equally well with hypertext versions (Monk *et al.*'s second study) suggests that such problems can be overcome. How performance would be altered with experience is an obvious question for further research.

Hypertext versus hypertext
Several studies have compared different implementations of hypertext documents to observe the effects of various organising principles or access mechanisms on performance. This is an important area. The term hypertext does not refer to a unitary concept. When comparisons are said to be made between hypertext and paper documents they are really being made between certain implementations of hypertext and standard versions of paper texts. Each implementation consists of one designer's (or group of designers') ideas about how to build the interface between users and information. To make general claims or draw conclusions about the wider relevance of hypertext in such circumstances is problematic. However, studies comparing varying implementations can shed some light on what constitutes good hypertext.

Simpson and McKnight (1990), for example, created eight versions of a hypertext document on plants, manipulating the contents list (hierarchical or alphabetic), presence or absence of a current position indicator and presence or absence of typographic cues. Subjects (researchers and students) were required to read the text until they felt confident they had seen it all and were then required to perform 10 information location tasks before attempting to construct a map of the document structure with cards. Results showed that readers using a hierarchical contents list navigated through the text more efficiently and produced more accurate maps of its structure than readers using an alphabetic index. The current position indicator and additional typographic cues were of limited utility.

Wright and Lickorish (1990) compared two types of navigation system for two different hypertexts. The navigation systems were termed Index navigation where the reader needed to return to a separate listing to specify where to move next, and Page navigation where the reader could jump directly to other "pages" from the current display. The two texts were on house-plants and supermarket prices. Twenty-four subjects read both hypertexts, 12 per navigation system, answering multiple-choice questions with the plants text and a variety of 'GoTo', compare and compute tasks with the supermarket text.

From their results they concluded that each navigation system had certain advantages in particular situations. For example, the paging navigation system may appear burdensome but was found to be beneficial with the house-plants text as it coupled navigation decisions with an overview of the text's structure. However, such activity with the tasks performed on the supermarket text (where decisions about where to go were not an issue because the questions provided such information) turned out to be an extra load on working memory. As Wright and Lickorish state, "authors need to bear in mind both the structure inherent in the content material and the tasks readers will be seeking to accomplish when they are designing navigation systems for hypertext."

Conclusions

Despite the claims frequently made for hypertext, experimental comparisons reveal that it is no guarantee of better performance, be it measured in terms of speed, comprehension, range of material covered or problems solved. Some hypertext implementations are good, some bad. Hypertext has advantages when readers are performing certain tasks with particular texts but offers no benefit, or is in fact worse than paper, in others. This is not too surprising. We should not expect any one implementation to be superior to all paper documents. After all, the diversity of textual documentation exists in the main for a purpose, i.e., to support the reader. Furthermore, as readers we all have a wealth of experience in dealing with paper texts which once learned, we apply effortlessly to our dealings with paper. Such experience, be it in the form of models of structure, rapid manipulation skills or accurate memory for location of items in a document, is often overlooked rather than exploited by developers of hypertexts. As the technology improves, any differences based on image quality should disappear; as readers become more experienced with hypertext, initial cognitive intrusion effects should be overcome. However, there are still many other problems to be addressed before hypertext will be exploited fully. The main point to take from this chapter is that users, tasks and texts vary tremendously and only by understanding the interaction of these three aspects of document usage can real progress be made.

CHAPTER FOUR

NAVIGATION THROUGH COMPLEX INFORMATION SPACES

"He that travelleth into a country before he hath entrance into the language, goeth to school, not to travel."

Bacon: Of Travel

With the advent of hypertext it has become widely accepted that the departure from the so-called 'linear' structure of paper increases the likelihood of readers or users becoming lost. In this chapter we will discuss this aspect of hypertext in terms of its validity, the lessons to be learned from the psychology of navigation, and the manner in which good design can minimise such problems for users of hypertext documents.

Is navigation a problem?

There is a striking consensus among many of the 'experts' in the field that navigation is the single greatest difficulty for users of hypertext. Frequent reference is made to "getting lost in hyperspace" (e.g., Conklin, 1987; McAleese, 1989a) which is described, in the oft-quoted line of Elm and Woods (1985), as:

> "the user not having a clear conception of the relationships within the system or knowing his present location in the system relative to the display structure and finding it difficult to decide where to look next within the system." (p.927)

In other words, users do not know how the information is organised, how to find the information they seek, or even if that information is available. With paper documents there tends to be at least some standards in terms of organisation. With books, for example, contents pages are usually at the front, indices at the back and both offer some information on where items are located in the body of the text. Concepts of relative position in the text such as 'before' and 'after' have tangible physical correlates. No such correlation holds with hypertext.

There is some direct empirical evidence in the literature to support the view that navigation in hypertext can be a problem.[1] Edwards and Hardman (1989), for example, describe a study which required subjects to search through a specially designed hypertext. In total, half the subjects reported feeling lost at some stage.[2] Such feelings were mainly due to "not knowing where to go next" or "not knowing where they were in relation to the overall structure of the document" rather than "knowing where to go but not knowing how to get there" (descriptors provided by the authors). Unfortunately, without direct comparison of ratings from subjects reading a paper equivalent we cannot be sure such proportions are solely due to using hypertext. However it is unlikely that many readers of paper texts do not know where they are in relation to the rest of the text![3]

Indirect evidence comes from the numerous studies which have indicated that users have difficulties with a hypertext (e.g., many of the studies cited in the previous chapter). Hammond and Allinson (1989) speak for many when they say:

> "Experience with using hypertext systems has revealed a number of problems for users...First, users get lost...Second, users may find it difficult to gain an overview of the material...Third, even if users know specific information is present they may have difficulty finding it." (p.294)

There are a few dissenting voices.[4] Brown (1989) argues that:

> "although getting lost is often claimed to be a great problem, the evidence is largely circumstantial and conflicting. In some smallish applications it is not a major problem at all." (p.2)

This quote is telling in several ways. The evidence for navigational difficulties *is*

---

[1] Interestingly there is significantly less evidence than there are claims about navigation difficulties. Whether this reflects a view that navigation is such an obvious problem that it is not worth demonstrating or an over-willing acceptance of it as a problem on the basis of limited evidence is open to argument.

[2] This proportion is deduced from the data reported.

[3] This descriptor has a certain ambiguity that confuses the issue. Positionally it is easy for readers to know where they are in terms of the front, back or middle of the book. The same relationship is much more complex when we consider "where am I?" in relation to the argument.

[4] At a recent international workshop on hypermedia, a well-known figure in the area stated emphatically during his presentation that "there is no navigation problem"! Unfortunately he neither produced evidence to support this statement nor repeated it in his written paper.

often circumstantial, as noted above. The applications in which Brown claims it is not a problem at all, are, to use his word, "smallish" and this raises an important issue with respect to hypertext. When we speak of documents being so small that a reader cannot 'get lost' in them or so large that navigation aids are required to use them effectively, the implication is that information occupies "space" through which readers 'travel' or 'move'. Hammond and Allinson (1987) talk of the "travel metaphor" as a way of moving through a hypertext. Canter *et al.* (1985) speak of "routes through" a database. Even the dissenters believe that the reader or user navigates through the document, the only disagreement being the extent to which getting lost is a regular and/or serious occurrence.

The weight of evidence, be it experiential, anecdotal or empirical suggests that navigation is an issue worthy of consideration. In the following section we will discuss what is known about the psychology of navigation in physical environments and show how this might have relevance to the 'virtual' worlds of information space.

The psychology of navigation

Surprisingly, for an activity that is routinely performed by all of us, navigation is not a well-studied psychological phenomenon in the same way that reading is. However, aspects relevant to the study of navigation are dealt with in some studies of spatial imagery, orientation, distance judgement and so forth. It is difficult to make a cohesive theory out of these disparate strands but some agreements do exist.

Schemata and models of generic environments

It seems obvious, for example, that we have a schema or model of the physical environment in which we find ourselves. This is acquired from experience and affords us a basic orienting frame of reference for navigatory purposes. Thus, we soon acquire schemata of towns and cities so that we know what to expect when we find ourselves in one: busy roads, numerous buildings, shopping, residential and industrial areas, many people, churches, pubs, and so on. According to Downs and Stea (1977), such frames of reference exist at all levels of scale from looking at the world in terms of east and west or First and Third Worlds, to national distinctions between north and south, urban and rural and so on down to local entities like buildings and neighbourhoods. It is precisely such models that give rise to powerful stereotypes encapsulated in the phrase "when you've seen one slum, you've seen them all" (for which 'slum' could be replaced with city, factory, church or whatever physical structure the speaker was dismissing).

Such frames of reference also guide our responses to the environment in terms of how we should behave. Therefore we soon realise that to interact effectively with an urban environment (e.g., to get from A to B) there are probably a variety of information sources available to us such as maps, street signs, landmarks, tourist information facilities and so forth. Roads must be crossed in certain ways, e.g., at pedestrian crossings or when there is no traffic, and you must pay if you want to use public transport. In this sense the frame of reference is identical to the concept of script (Schank and Abelson, 1976) mentioned in the previous chapter.

While schemata are effective orienting guides, in themselves they are limited. They do not reflect specific instances of any one environment and provide no knowledge of what exists outside of our field of vision. Yet humans have such knowledge of places with which they are familiar. We know our houses well enough to walk through them mentally and describe objects and colours we encounter. Schemata or frames would allow us to predict that any one house contains a kitchen towards the back or bedrooms and a bathroom upstairs, for example, but as such this would be an expectancy rather than knowledge. We could only guess at colours and objects we might find. With cities, a schema might tell us that there are numerous routes to the same place but would not enable us to describe one or predict the shortest. However, individuals who live in that city would be able to describe the routes and accurately predict their respective journey times. So what is this detailed knowledge that we acquire of our environment, and how does it emerge?

The acquisition of cognitive maps
Current theories of navigation vary and the topic is no longer the province of psychologists alone. Geographers, anthropologists and urban planners all show an interest (see, for example, Downs and Stea, 1973). However, Tolman's (1948) paper on cognitive maps is frequently cited as seminal. True, this paper describes a number of studies on rats travelling through mazes (a constant source of amusement to those who feel that academic psychology has little relevance to real life!), but in it Tolman discusses the implications of this work for human cognition and postulates the existence of a cognitive map, internalised in the human mind, which is the analogue to the physical lay-out of the environment. In dismissing much of the then popular behaviouristic school of psychology, Tolman argues that information impinging on the brain is:

> "worked over and elaborated...into a tentative cognitive-like map of the environment indicating routes and paths and environmental relationships..."

Over 40 years later, such a perspective is readily accepted and the nonpsychologists among us might even wonder how such an obvious statement could ever have caused controversy. Recent experimental work takes the notion of some form of mental representation of the environment for granted, concerning itself more with how such maps are formed and manipulated. Many theorists agree that the acquisition of navigational knowledge proceeds through several developmental stages from the initial identification of landmarks in the environment to a fully formed mental map. One such developmental model has been discussed by Anderson (1980) and Wickens (1984) and is briefly described here.

According to this model, in the first instance we represent knowledge in terms of highly salient visual *landmarks* in the environment such as buildings, statues, etc. Thus we recognise our position in terms relative to these landmarks, e.g., our destination is near building X, or if we see statue Y then we must be near the railway station, and so forth. This knowledge provides us with the skeletal framework on which we build our cognitive map.

The next stage of development is the acquisition of *route* knowledge which is characterised by the ability to navigate from point A to point B, using whatever landmark knowledge we have acquired to make decisions about when to turn left or right. With such knowledge we can provide others with effective route guidance, e.g., "Turn left at the traffic lights and continue on that road until you see the Bull's Head public house on your left, and take the next right there..." and so forth. Though possessing route knowledge, a person may still not really know much about his environment. A route might be non-optimal or even totally wasteful.

The third stage involves the acquisition of *survey* knowledge. This is the fully developed cognitive map that Tolman described. It allows us to give directions or plan journeys along routes we have not directly travelled as well as describe relative locations of landmarks within an environment. It allows us to know the general direction of places, e.g., "westward" or "over there" rather than "left of the main road" or "to the right of the church". In other words, it is based on a world frame of reference rather than an ego-centred one.

It is not clear if each individual develops through all stages in such a logical sequence. Obviously, landmark knowledge on its own is of little use for complex navigation, and both route and survey knowledge emerge from it as a means of coping with the complexity of the environment. However, it does not necessarily follow that once enough route knowledge is acquired it is replaced by survey knowledge. Experimental investigations have demonstrated that each is optimally suited for different kinds of tasks. For example, route knowledge is better for orientation tasks than survey knowledge, the latter being better for estimating distance or object localisation on a map (Thorndyke and Hayes-Roth, 1982; Wetherell, 1979). Route knowledge is cognitively simpler than survey knowledge but suffers the drawback of being virtually useless once a wrong step is taken (Wickens, 1984). Route knowledge, because of its predominantly verbal form, might suit individuals with higher verbal than spatial abilities, while the opposite would be the case for survey knowledge.

Conclusions

While such theoretical work on navigation is primarily concerned with travels through physical space such as cities and buildings, it does offer a perspective that might prove insightful to the design of hypertext systems where navigation is conceptualised as occurring through an information space. In an attempt to relate the discussion of navigation to more directly relevant issues the following section details what is known about navigation through paper documents.

Navigation applied to paper documents

Schemata and models

When we pick up a book, we immediately have access to a whole host of information about the likely contents, its size, subject matter and so forth. Even looking at just the book cover tells us a lot about the likely style of coverage and so forth. When we open the book, we have expectations about what we will find inside the front cover such as details of where and when it was published, perhaps a dedication, and then a contents page. We know, for example, that contents listings describe the layout of the book in terms of chapters, proceeding from the front to the back. Chapters are organised around themes, and an index at the back of the book, organised alphabetically, provides more specific information on where information is located in the body of the text. Experienced readers know all this before even opening the text. It would strike us as odd if such structures were absent or their positions within the text were altered, e.g., the contents page was at the back or in the middle, there were no chapter divisions, or the index was not arranged alphabetically.

The same might be said of a newspaper. Typically we might expect a section on the previous day's political news at home, foreign coverage, market developments and so forth. News of sport will be grouped together in a distinct section and there will also be a section covering that evening's television and radio schedules. The same is probably true for most text types, i.e., there are organisational principles governing the lay-out and structure of their contents.

Some of the most impressive work in this area has been carried out by van Dijk and Kintsch (1983). We noted in the previous chapter how they have proposed a model of discourse comprehension that involves readers analysing the propositions of a text and forming a macropropositional hierarchy. According to this theory, readers acquire (through experience) schemata (which van Dijk and Kintsch term 'superstructures') that facilitate comprehension of material by allowing readers to predict the likely ordering and grouping of constituent elements of a body of text. To quote van Dijk (1980):

> "a superstructure is the schematic form that organises the global meaning of a text. We assume that such a superstructure consists of functional categories...(and)...rules that specify which category may follow or combine with what other categories." (p.108)

Apart from categories and functional rules, van Dijk adds that a superstructure must be socio-culturally accepted, learned, used and commented upon by most adult language users of a speech community.

They have applied this theory to several text types. For example, with respect to newspaper articles they describe a schema consisting of headlines and leads (which together provide a summary), major event categories each of which is placed within a context (actual or historical), and consequences. Depending on the type of newspaper (e.g., weekly as opposed to daily) we might expect elaborated commentaries and evaluations. Experiments by Kintsch and Yarborough (1982) showed that articles written in a way that adhered to this schema resulted in better grasp of the main ideas and subject matter than ones which were re-organised to make them less schema-conforming. When given a cloze test[5] of the articles, no difference was observed. The authors suggest that schematic structures are not particularly relevant as far as ability to remember specific details such as words is concerned, but have major importance at the macropropositional level of comprehension.

At a more global level, two studies by Dillon (1990a) tested readers' ability to impose structure on paragraphs and sentences of text. In the first study, subjects were given paragraphs from academic journal articles and asked to organise them into one article as fast as they could. To avoid referential continuity, every second paragraph was removed. In one condition headings were provided, in the other they were absent. The results indicated that readers had little difficulty piecing the article together into gross categories of Introduction, Method, Results and Discussion (over 80% accuracy at this level) but had difficulties distinguishing the precise order at the within-section level. When provided with headings, subjects

---

5   A cloze test is a traditional comprehension test for readers that requires them to fill in the blanks on sentences taken from the text they have just read.

formed the same major categories but were less accurate in placing second level headings in the correct section. This suggests that experienced journal readers are capable of distinguishing isolated paragraphs of text according to their likely location within a complete article with respect to the major categories. Interestingly, this could be done without resorting to reading every word or attempting to understand the subject matter of the paper.[6]

In the second study, subjects read a selection of paragraphs from two articles on both paper and screen and had to place each one in the general section to which they thought it belonged (Introduction, Method, Results or Discussion). Again, subjects showed a high degree of accuracy (over 80%) with the only advantage to paper being speed (subjects were significantly faster at the 5% level in the paper condition) which is probably explicable in terms of image quality variables, as outlined in the previous chapter. Taken together, these results suggest that readers do have a model of the typical journal article that allows them to gauge accurately where certain information is located. This model does not seem to be affected by presentation medium.

In this format, the model/schema/superstructure constitutes a set of expectancies about their usual contents and how these are grouped and positioned relative to each other. Obviously, in advance of actually reading the text we cannot have much insight into anything more specific than this, but the generality of organisation within the multitude of texts we read in everyday life affords stability and orientation in what could otherwise be an over-complex informational environment.

Acquiring a cognitive map of the text

If picking up a new book can be compared to a stranger entering a new town (i.e., we know what each is like on the basis of previous experience and have expectancies of what we will find), how do we proceed to develop our map of the information space?

To use the analogy of navigation in physical space, we would expect that generic structures such as indices, contents, chapter headings and summaries, page numbers and so forth would be seen as landmarks that provide readers with information about where they are in a text, just as signposts, buildings and street names aid navigation in physical environments. Thus, when initially reading a text, we might notice that there are numerous figures and diagrams in certain sections, none in others, or that a very important point or detail is raised in a section

---

6   Subjects were asked to note down what they thought each article was about after each condition but most had only vague notions based on keywords and phrases observed, even though the articles were in their general area of expertise.

containing a table of numerical values. In fact, readers often claim to experience such a sense of knowing where an item of information occurred in the body of the text even if they cannot recall that item precisely, and there is some empirical evidence to suggest that this is in fact the case.

Rothkopf (1971) carried out an experiment to test whether such occurrences had a basis in reality rather than resulting from popular myth supported by chance success. He asked people to read a 12 page extract from a book with the intention of answering questions on content afterwards. What subjects didn't realise was that they would be asked to recall the location of information in the text in terms of its occurrence both within the page (divided into eighths) and the complete text (divided into quarters). The results showed that incidental memory for locations within any page and within the text as a whole was more accurate than chance, i.e., people could remember location information even though they were not asked to. There was also a positive correlation between location of information at the within-page level and accuracy of question answering.

There have been several follow-up studies by Rothkopf and by other investigators into this phenomenon. Zechmeister and McKillip (1972) had subjects read eight pages of text typed into blocks with four blocks per page. Subjects were asked to read the text before being tested on it. The test consisted of fill-in-the-blank questions, confidence ratings on the answers, and location of the answer on the page. Again, an effect for knowledge of location was observed which was correlated to accuracy of answers, suggesting that memory for location and for content are independent attributes of memory that can be linked for mnemonic purposes. Interestingly, no interaction of memory for location and confidence in answer was found. Further work by Zechmeister *et al.* (1975) and by Lovelace and Southall (1983) confirm the view that memory for spatial location within in body of text is reliable even if it is generally limited.[7]

The analogy with navigation in a physical environment is of limited applicability beyond the level of landmark knowledge. Given the fact that the information space is instantly accessible to the reader (i.e., he can open a text at any point), the necessity for route knowledge, for example, is lessened (if not eliminated). To get from point A to point B in a text is not dependent on taking the correct course in the same way that it is in a physical three-dimensional environment. The reader can jump ahead (or back), guess, use the index or contents or just page serially through the text. Readers rarely rely on just one route

---

7   In psychology, to describe a phenomenon as "reliable" implies that it is a non-chance occurrence. The implication in this context is that readers do indeed have memory for spatial location of information within a text but that it does not exist for all information. Thus, it is reliable but limited.

or get confused if they have to start from a different point in the text in order to go to the desired location, as would be the case if route knowledge was a formal stage in their development of navigational knowledge for texts. Once you know the page number of an item you can get there as you like. Making an error is not as costly as it is in the physical world either in terms of time or effort. Furthermore, few texts are used in such a way as to *require* that level or type of knowledge.

A similar case can be made with respect to survey knowledge. While it seems likely that a reader experienced with a certain text can mentally envisage where information is in the body of the text, what cross-references are relevant to his purpose and so forth, we must be careful that we are still talking of navigation and not changing the level of discourse to how the argument is developed in the text or the ordering in which points are made. Without doubt, such knowledge exists, but often it is not purely navigational knowledge but an instantiation of several schemata such as domain knowledge of the subject matter, interpretation of the author's argument, and a sense of how this knowledge is organised that come into play now. This is not to say that readers cannot possess survey-type knowledge of a text's contents; rather, it is to highlight the limitations of directly mapping concepts from one domain to another on the basis of terminology alone.

The fact that we use the term navigation in both situations does not mean that they are identical activities with similar patterns of development. The simple differences in applying findings from a three-dimensional world (with visual, olfactory, auditory and powerful tactile stimuli) to a two-dimensional text (with visual and limited tactile stimuli only) and the varying purposes to which such knowledge is put in either domain are bound to have a limiting effect.

It might be that, rather than route and survey knowledge, a reader develops a more elaborated analogue model of the text based on the skeletal framework of landmark knowledge outlined earlier. Thus, as familiarity with the text grows, the reader becomes more familiar with the various landmarks in the text and their inter-relationships. In effect the reader builds a representation of the text similar to the survey knowledge of physical environments without any intermediary route knowledge but in a form that is directly representative of the text rather than physical domain.

The manner in which knowledge is represented mentally is a fundamental issue in cognitive psychology and one which we will not delve deeply into here. Suffice to acknowledge that various representational forms exist and the distinctive nature of navigation in text compared to physical environments is sufficient to require alternative representations.

Navigation applied to electronic documents

Schemata and models

The concept of a schema for an electronic information space is less clear-cut than those for physical environments or paper documents. Electronic documents have a far shorter history than paper and the level of awareness of technology among the general public is relatively primitive compared to that of paper. Exposure to information technology will almost certainly improve this state of affairs, but even among the contemporary computer-literate it is unlikely that the type of generic schematic structures that exist for paper documents have electronic equivalents of sufficient generality.[8]

Obviously, computing technology's short history is one of the reasons why this might be so, but it is also the case that the media's underlying structures do not have equivalent transparency. With paper, once the basic *modus operandi* of reading are acquired (e.g., page-turning, footnote identification, index usage and so forth) they retain utility for other texts produced by other publishers, other authors and for other domains. With computers, manipulation of information can differ from application to application within the same computer, from computer to computer, and from this year's to last year's model. Thus, using electronic information is often likely to involve the employment of schemata for systems in general (i.e., how to operate them) in a way that is not essential for paper-based information.

The qualitative differences between the schemata for paper and electronic documents can easily be appreciated by considering what you can tell about either at first glance. We have outlined the information available to paper text users in the section on paper schemata above. When we open a hypertext document, however, we do not have the same amount of information available to us. We are likely to be faced with a welcoming screen which might give us a rough idea of the contents (i.e., subject matter) and information about the authors/developers of the document, but little else. It is two-dimensional, gives no indication of size, quality of contents, age (unless explicitly stated) or how frequently it has been used (i.e., there is no dust or signs of wear and tear on it such as grubby finger-marks or underlines and scribbled comments). At the electronic document level, there is usually no way of telling even the relative size without performing some 'query operation'. For example, in Figure 9, is the 'WineBook' bigger or smaller than

---

8 It is worth noting that in part, this might be because the electronic document is usually only a stage in the production of a paper one. Few pure electronic texts exist, thus any unique forms have yet to emerge.

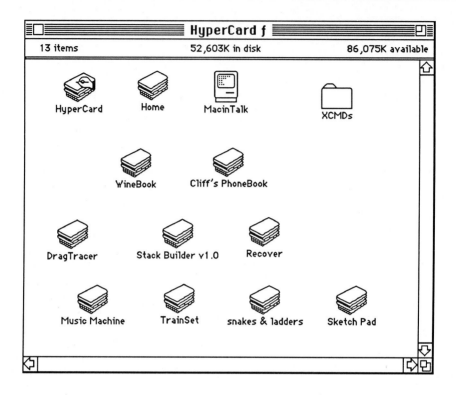

Figure 9: Electronic documents give no obvious clues to their size.

'Cliff's PhoneBook'? Without using the 'Get Info' command on both and comparing their sizes (given in kilobytes), there is no way of telling.

Performing the hypertext equivalent of opening up the text or turning the page offers no assurance that expectations will be met. Many hypertext documents offer unique structures (intentionally or otherwise) and their overall sizes are often impossible to assess in a meaningful manner (McKnight *et al.*, 1989b). At the current stage of development, it is likely that users or readers familiar with hypertext will have a schema that includes such attributes as linked nodes of information, non-serial structures, and perhaps even potential navigational difficulties! The manipulation facilities and access mechanisms available in hypertext will probably occupy a more prominent rôle in their schemata for hypertext documents than they will for readers' schemata of paper texts. As yet, empirical evidence for such schemata is lacking.

The fact that hypertext offers authors the chance to create numerous structures out of the same information is a further source of difficulty for users or readers.

Since schemata are generic abstractions representing typicality in entities or events, the increased variance of hypertext implies that any similarities that are perceived must be at a higher level or must be more numerous than the schemata that exist for paper texts.

It seems, therefore, that users' schemata of hypertext environments are likely to be 'informationally leaner' than those for paper documents. This is attributable to the recent emergence of electronic documents and comparative lack of experience interacting with them as opposed to paper texts for even the most dedicated users. The lack of standards in the electronic domain compared to the rather traditional structures of many paper documents is a further problem for schema development at this point in time.

Acquiring a cognitive map of the electronic space
As mentioned above, navigation through hypertext is considered a major issue by many designers and researchers. The roots of this issue lie in the literature on users interacting with non-hypertext databases and documents as well as with menu-driven interfaces, where it has been repeatedly shown that users can lose their way in the maze of information.

Hagelbarger and Thompson (1983) claim that when users make an incorrect selection at a deep level they tend to return to the start rather than the menu at which they erred. Research by Tombaugh and McEwen (1982) and Lee *et al.* (1984) indicates that the actual to minimum ratio for screens of information accessed in a successful search is 2:1, i.e., users will often access twice as many menu pages as necessary. These findings led researchers to conclude that navigation through electronic (but non-hypertext) databases can pose severe navigational problems for users.

A relevant variable in navigation through menus is the method of classifying the information available in the database, i.e., how the information space is organised. Barnard *et al.* (1977) demonstrated that the manner of classification (such as whether it was alphabetical or relational) influenced the time taken to access targets in a menu-style task. They conclude, not surprisingly perhaps, that the users' conceptualisation of the desired information influences the selections they make *en route*. Research by Snowberry *et al.* (1985) indicates that the main source of difficulty is the relatively weak associations which users have between category descriptors at the highest level of menu and the desired information at the lower level, i.e., there is little information in the immediate environment that aids users' navigation decisions. This is a fault of design where little attempt is made to identify the end-user's conceptualisation of the information space. Significantly enough, Lee *et al.* (1984) discovered considerable variation among experts in terms of what they believe constitutes a "good" or well-organised menu.

In terms of the model of navigational knowledge described above, we should not be surprised by such findings. They seem to be classic manifestations of behaviour based on limited knowledge. For example, returning to the start upon making an error at a deep level in the menu suggests the absence of survey type knowledge and a strong reliance on landmarks (e.g., the start screen) to guide navigation. It also lends support to the argument about route knowledge, that it becomes useless once a wrong turn is made. Making 'journeys' twice as long as necessary is a further example of the the type of behaviour expected from people lacking a mental map of an environment and relying on only landmark and route knowledge to find their way.

Jones and Dumais (1986) empirically tested spatial memory over symbolic memory for application in the electronic domain, citing the work of Rothkopf and others as indicators that such memory might be important. In a series of three experiments, they had subjects simulate filing and retrieval operations using name, location or a combination of both stimuli as cues. Like the preceding work on texts, they found that memory for location is above chance but modest compared to memory for names and concluded that it may be of limited utility for object reference in the electronic domain.

Therefore, we know that navigational difficulties exist where users need to make decisions about location in an electronic information space. There seems to be some evidence that the first stage of knowledge about navigation is of the landmark variety and that the organising principles on which the information structure is built are important. We now turn to the more specific evidence for hypertext.

Acquiring a cognitive map of a hypertext document
The study by McKnight *et al.* (1990) described in the previous chapter looked at navigation in terms of the amount of time spent in the contents and/or index sections of the documents employed. They found that subjects in both hypertext conditions spent significantly greater proportions of time in the index/contents sections of the documents. We noted that this indicated a style of interaction based on jumping into parts of the text and returning to 'base' for further guidance — a style assumed not particularly optimal for hypertext — and concluded from this that effective navigation was difficult for non-experienced users of a hypertext document.

Once more this is an example of using landmarks in the information space as guidance. Subjects in the linear conditions (paper and word processor versions) seemed much happier to browse through the document to find information, highlighting their confidence and familiarity with the structure presented to them.

Similar support for the notion of landmarks as a first level of navigational knowledge development are provided by several of the studies which have required subjects to draw or form maps of the information space after exposure to it (e.g., Simpson and McKnight, 1990). Typically, subjects can group certain sections together but often have no idea where other parts go or what they are connected to.

Unfortunately it is difficult to chart the development of navigational knowledge beyond this point. Detailed studies of users interacting with hypertext systems beyond single experimental tasks and gaining mastery over a hypertext document are thin on the ground. Edwards and Hardman (1989) claim that they found evidence for the development of survey type navigational knowledge in users exposed to a strictly hierarchical database of fifty screens for a single experimental session lasting, on average, less than 20 minutes. Unfortunately the data are not reported in sufficient detail to allow a critical assessment of such a claim, but it is possible that, given the document's highly organised structure, comparatively small size and the familiarity of the subject area (leisure facilities in Edinburgh), such knowledge might have been observed. Obviously this is an area that needs further empirical work.

While it is clear that empirical work on hypertext is limited, numerous designers and researchers have considered the navigation issues in less experimental ways, without concerning themselves with the development of mental representations of the information space. In the following section we discuss the two major themes to have emerged from this work: the design of suitable maps, browsers and landmarks for users, and the concept of metaphor provision to aid navigation.

Providing navigational information: browsers, maps and structural cues
A graphical browser is a schematic representation of the structure of a hypertext aimed at providing the user with an easy-to-understand map of where particular information is located. According to Conklin (1987), graphical browsers are a feature of a "somewhat idealized hypertext system", recognising that not all existing systems utilise browsers but suggesting that they are desirable. A typical browser is shown in Figure 10. The idea behind a browser is that the document can be represented graphically in terms of the nodes of information and the links between them and, in some instances, that selecting a node in the browser would cause its information to be displayed.

It is not difficult to see why this might be useful. Like a map of a physical environment, it shows the user what the overall information space is like, how it is linked together and consequently offers a means of moving from one information node to another. Indeed, Monk *et al.* (1988) have shown that even a static, non-

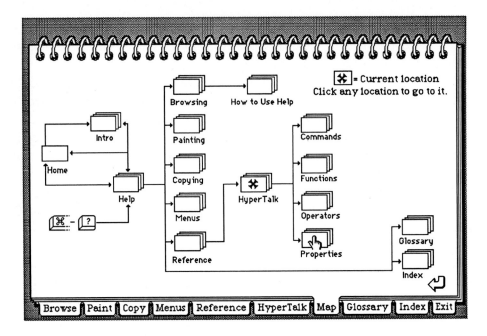

Figure 10: A graphical browser from Apple's HyperCard Help stack.

interactive graphical representation is useful. However, for richly interconnected material or documents of a reasonable size and complexity, it is not possible to include everything in a single browser without the problem of presenting 'visual spaghetti' to the user. In such cases it is necessary to represent the structure in terms of levels of browsers, and at this point there is a danger that the user gets lost in the navigational support system!

Some simple variations in the form of maps or browsers have been investigated empirically. In a non-hypertext environment, Billingsley (1982) had subjects select information from a database aided by an alphabetical list of selection numbers, a map of the database structure or no aid. The map proved superior, with the no aid group performing worst.

In the hypertext domain, a number of studies by Simpson (1989) have experimentally manipulated several variables relating to structural cues and position indicators. Her subjects performed a series of tasks on articles about house-plants and herbs. In one experiment she found that a hierarchical contents list was superior to an alphabetic index and concluded that users are able to use cues from the structural representation to form maps of the document. In a second study she reported that users provided with a graphical contents list showing the relationship between various parts of the text performed better than users who only had access to a textual list. Making the contents lists interactive (i.e., selectable by pointing) also increased navigational efficiency.

Manipulating 'last card seen' markers produced mixed results. It might be expected that such a cue would be advantageous to all users, but Simpson reported that this cue seemed of benefit only during initial familiarisation periods and for users of non-interactive contents lists. Further experiments revealed that giving users a record of the items they had seen aided navigation, much as would be expected from the literature on physical navigation which assumes that knowledge of current position is built on knowledge of how you arrived there (Canter, 1984). In general, Simpson found that as accuracy of performance increased so did subjects' ability to construct accurate post-task maps of the information space.

Such work is important to designers of hypertext systems. It represents a useful series of investigations into how 'contents pages' for hypertext documents should be designed. Admittedly, it concerned limited tasks in a small information space, but such studies are building blocks for a better understanding of the important issues in designing hypertext systems. As always, however, more research needs to be done.

The provision of metaphors

A second area of research in the domain of navigational support concerns that of metaphor provision. A metaphor offers a way of conceptualising an object or environment and in the information technology domain is frequently discussed as a means for aiding novices' comprehension of a system or application. The most common metaphor in use is the desk-top metaphor familiar to users of the Apple Macintosh among others. Here, the user is presented with a virtual desktop on-screen and can perform routine file manipulations by opening and closing 'folders' and 'documents' and throwing them in the 'wastepaper bin' to delete them. Prior to this metaphor, the word processor was often conceptualised by first-time users as a typewriter.[9]

The logic behind metaphors is that they enable users to draw on existing world knowledge in order to act on the electronic domain. As Carroll and Thomas (1982) point out:

> "If people employ metaphors in learning about computing systems, the designers of those systems should anticipate and support likely

---

9 The history of technological progress is littered with such metaphors, e.g., the car as a "horseless carriage", the first typefaces were imitations of script, and so on.

metaphorical constructions to increase the ease of learning and using the system."

However, rather than anticipate likely metaphorical constructions, the general approach in the domain of hypertext has been to provide a metaphor and hope (or examine the extent to which) the user can employ it. As the term navigation suggests, the most commonly provided metaphor is that of travel.

Hammond and Allinson (1987) report on a study in which two different forms of the travel metaphor were employed: 'go-it-alone' travel, and the 'guided tour'. These two forms were intended to represent different loci of control over movement through the document, the first being largely user-controlled and the second being largely system-controlled. Additionally, a map of the local part of the information structure was available from every screen, with selectable arrows at the four edges leading to further maps, frames so far visited indicated, and all frames directly selectable from the map. Hammond and Allinson stress the importance of integrating the metaphor in the design of the system, which they did, and not surprisingly they found that users were able to employ it with little difficulty.

Of course, one could simply make the electronic book look as similar to the paper book as possible. This is the approach offered by people such as Benest (1990) with his book emulator and as such seems to offer a simple conceptual aid to novice users. Two pages are displayed at a time and relative position within the text can be assessed by the thickness of pages either side which are splayed out rather like a paper document would be. Page turning can be done with a single mouse press, which results in two new pages appearing, or by holding the mouse button down and simulating 'flicking' through the text. The layout of typical books can also be supported by such a system, thereby exploiting the schematic representations which we know that experienced readers possess.

If that was all such a system offered it would be unlikely to succeed; it would just be a second-rate book. However, according to Benest, his book emulator provides added-value that exploits the technology underlying it. For example, although references in the text are listed fully at the back of the book, they can be individually accessed by pointing at them when they occur on screen. Page numbers in contents and index sections are also selectable, thereby offering immediate access to particular portions of the text. Such advantages are typical of most hypertext applications. In his own words:

"the book presentation, with all the engrained expectations that it arouses and the simplicity with which it may be navigated, is both visually appealing and less disruptive during information acquisition, than the older 'new medium demands a new approach' techniques that have so far been adopted."

This may be true, but at the time of writing no supporting evidence has been presented and as we have noted earlier, in the absence of empirical data one should view all claims about hypertext with caution.

It is interesting for two reasons that Benest dismisses the 'new medium demands a new approach' philosophy of most hypertext theorists. Firstly, there is a good case to be made for book-type emulations according to the arguments put forward above about the schematic representations which readers possess of texts. As outlined earlier, such representations facilitate usage by providing orientation or frames of reference for naïve users. Such points have been raised in sufficient detail earlier not to require further elaboration here. Secondly, the new approach which rejects such emulations has largely been responsible for the adoption of the concept of navigation through hypertext.

In response to the first issue it is worth noting that Benest's approach is, to our way of thinking, correct up to a point. We ourselves have been developing a hypertext journal database and have decided that, on the basis of some of our studies cited earlier on usage styles and models of academic articles, emulating the structure of the journal as it exists in paper is good design. However, we are less concerned with emulation as much as retention of useful structures. This does not extend as far as mimicking page-turning or providing splayed images of the pages underlying either opened leaf. Furthermore, while we advocate the approach of identifying relevant schematic structures for texts, we would not expect all types to retain such detailed aspects of their paper versions in hypertext. There seems little need, for example, to emulate the book form to this degree for a hypertext telephone directory. Benest does not seem to draw the line however between texts that might usefully exploit such emulations and those that would not, or state what he would expect unique hypertext documents to emulate.

In response to the second point, it is worth asking 'is there an alternative to navigation as a metaphor'? As we have continually noted in this chapter, the dominant approach to hypertext has produced the navigation-through-space metaphor. Benest, though still talking of navigation, does so in the limited sense that it is used in the paper domain. The more typical hypertext approach embraces navigation whole-heartedly and uses it as a means of inducing orienting schemata in the user's mind.

Hammond and Allinson (1987) discuss the merits of the metaphor approach in general and the navigation one in particular for hypertext. They argue that there are two relevant dimensions for understanding the information which metaphors convey: *scope* and *level* of description. A metaphor's scope refers to the number of concepts that the metaphor relates to. A metaphor of broad scope in the domain of HCI is the desk-top metaphor common to many computing interfaces. Here, many of the concepts a user deals with when working on the system can be easily dealt with cognitively in terms of physical desk-top manipulations. The typewriter metaphor frequently invoked for explaining word processors is far more limited in scope. It offers a basic orientation to using word processors (i.e., you can use them to create print quality documents) but is severely limited beyond that as word processors do not behave like typewriters in many instances.

The metaphor's level of description refers to the type of knowledge it is intended to convey. This may be very high level information such as how to think about the task and its completion, or very low, such as how to think about particular command syntax in order to remember it easily. Hammond and Allinson talk of four levels: task, semantic, lexical and physical which refer to general issues such as: "Can I do it?"; "What does this command do?"; "What does that term mean?" and "What activities are needed to achieve that?" respectively. Few, if any, metaphors convey information at all levels, but this does not prevent them being useful to users. In fact, few users ever expect metaphors to offer full scope and levels of description.

According to Hammond and Allinson, the navigation metaphor is useful in the hypertext domain and when users are offered 'guided tours' through an information space they do not expect physical manifestations of the metaphor to apply literally but might rely primarily on semantic mappings between metaphor and system much more heavily. As we have attempted to outline in the present chapter, there are numerous rich mappings that can be made between the navigation metaphor and hypertext, and thus it seems sensible to use it.

Benest's book emulation is also a metaphor for using the system and in some instances would offer a broad scope and many levels of description between the paper text and the hypertext. The fact that we can talk about navigation and book metaphors in the one system shows that mixed metaphors are even possible and (though awaiting confirmatory evidence) probably workable in some instances.

It is hard to see any other metaphors being employed in this domain. Navigation is firmly entrenched as a metaphor for discussing hypertext use, and book comparisons are unavoidable in a technology aimed at supporting many of the tasks performed with paper documentation. Whether there are other metaphors that can be usefully employed is debatable. Limited metaphors for explaining computer use to the novice user are bound to exist, and where such users find themselves working with hypertext new metaphors might find their way into the domain. For now at least, though, it seems that navigation and book emulation are here to stay.

Navigating the semantic space

One aspect of the whole navigation issue that often appears overlooked in the hypertext literature is that of the semantic space of a text or electronic document. In other words, to what extent does a user or reader need to find his way about the *argument* that an author creates as opposed to, or distinct from, navigating through the *structure* of the information?

It is probably impossible to untangle these aspects completely. We noted earlier, in the section on readers' memory for spatial location on pages, that there was a correlation between memory for location and comprehension. This is attributed to the fact that they are independent aspects of memory which are capable of being linked for mnemonic purposes. In other words, memories may consist of a constellation of attributes in which the recall of any one attribute is facilitated by the recall of others.

In terms of hypertext it seems that the ability to navigate through the information space should in some sense be related to the user's comprehension of the contents of the document. At the time of writing, this question has not been directly tested. Most of the studies reported in this and the preceding chapter have contented themselves with looking at ability to locate information in a document rather than considering comprehension. It is not valid to infer that, because users can locate correct information or produce accurate maps of a hypertext's structure, they necessarily understand its contents. It is likely that readers who well understand a hypertext's contents will also have the ability to accurately locate information in it, but there is no guarantee that the reverse holds true.

Navigation through the semantic space will not relate or map absolutely to navigation in the structural sense if authors are not good at structuring information. It is conceivable that the linking power of hypertext packages will encourage some authors merely to link everything to everything else, or keep adding further nodes of information according to some vague philosophy which espouses association as 'natural' and hence desirable, leaving the reader to decide what they want to access. In such situations, grasping the message and grasping the structure will not necessarily overlap.

A further distinguishing characteristic is that while we can easily compare how near ideas are in terms of location in a structure, i.e., how many links exist between two nodes or the number of selections/button presses need to be made to access node Z from node A, we cannot offer a similar measure of semantic distance. The extent to which two ideas are related may seem intuitively easy to assess but is unlikely to have an agreed quantifiable metric (see, for example, the work of Osgood *et al*, 1957, and Kelly, 1955). The notion of structuring semantic space will be discussed further in the chapters on writing and education.

Conclusion

The concept of navigation is a meaningful one in the hypertext domain in the sense that we can view user actions as movement through electronic space. Research in the psychology of navigation in physical environments has some relevance but needs further empirical investigation to identify the extent to which the issues it raises may map directly onto users of electronic documents. Limitations in scope and level of such a mapping need to be made explicit. The expression of navigation difficulties is rarely supported with clear evidence however, and the need for sound empirical work here should not be underestimated. The psychological model of navigation knowledge could prove a useful research tool in these circumstances. With respect to navigation of semantic space, it seems that existing research has little to tell us and the onus is on workers in the area to gain an understanding of such concepts through their own work.

CHAPTER FIVE

CREATING HYPERTEXT

"Everything involves structural hierarchy...nothing can be understood without looking at it not only in isolation on its own level but also at both its internal structure and external relationships which simultaneously establish the larger structure and modify the smaller one."
C.S. Smith: Structural Hierarchy in Science, Art and History

Introduction

A current paradox of hypertext is that while there is considerable interest in the concept, and a number of fully implemented systems, there are few widely known hypertexts. The BBC Domesday videodisk project was certainly ambitious in terms of scope, but the high cost of the hardware restricted the uptake by individual schools and the patchy coverage limited the tasks for which the system was appropriate. Extensive experimental hypertexts have been developed in research and development departments in both the educational (Intermedia, Writing Environment) and private sector (KMS, Document Examiner, Thoth-II, NoteCards, gIBIS), but the market for 'published' hypertext has yet to take off. The vast majority of current hypertexts are small, with restricted functionality and of experimental interest rather than practical significance.[1] However, while most hypertext systems require advanced workstations and are therefore unavailable to many people, Apple has been including a copy of their HyperCard application with every new Macintosh computer since 1987, and OWL's Guide system for the Macintosh has been available since 1985 (see Brown, 1987). Thus, the means for popular hypertext are gradually appearing.

---

[1] A notable exception is the hypertext version of the *Engineering Data Compendium*, a reference encyclopædia of human factors knowledge written for designers and engineers. See Glushko (1989).

The situation described above contrasts sharply with Ted Nelson's vision of the 'Docuverse' which contains every text (past and present) in hypertext format, uniquely referenced, universally available and easily included in new hypertexts (see Nelson, 1988). This scenario, even if only achieved in part, is likely to be a long way off and the difficulties that would have to be overcome are considerable. In Chapter 7 we describe, as a case study, the design and creation of a hypertext scientific journal from a paper original — putting into practice some of the ideas discussed in the earlier chapters. In this chapter we shall consider some of the practical problems, which are capable of reasonably clear definition, and then some of the pedagogical issues connected with alternative ways of structuring information.

It is convenient, and in keeping with Nelson's ambitions, to consider the practical problems according to whether existing texts are being transformed into hypertext or whether completely original hypertext is being created.

The conversion of text into hypertext

The possible reasons why a text may be considered suitable for conversion to hypertext format include all those which apply to the creation of basic electronic texts. The advantages of electronic formats are most clearly seen in the improved access that they offer to texts. Thus, for example, many readers can access the same text immediately and simultaneously via a network; lengthy texts can be readily searched, edited and incorporated into new documents if desired; and version control can be managed with greater efficiency so that all readers can be confident that they are reading the most recent version of the text. A hypertext implementation not only enjoys all the above advantages but also offers the increased convenience afforded by the dynamic linking of the constituent elements and a greatly increased flexibility of design.

For the publishing community some significant problems will need to be addressed before electronic products are commonplace. For the publisher the potential market is still relatively small, there are problems in terms of incompatible hardware and software systems and, as yet, no proven techniques for protecting electronic texts from unauthorised reproduction.[2]

A major criticism of the Nelson vision has concerned the cost of the effort required to create hypertext versions of existing texts on a major scale. This view assumes that each text would need to be individually transformed, with each

---

2   The unauthorised photocopying of full length *printed* documents can often be as expensive as buying legitimate copies.

hypertext link uniquely specified. Although the effort required to convert texts into hypertext on any scale should not be underestimated,[3] there are a number of reasons why the task may not be as great as it first appears. These include the differing frequencies with which texts are accessed by readers, the rôle of machine-readable texts in the printing process, the nature of the transformation that will be appropriate, and the increasing use of generic text mark-up languages.

Text access frequencies

While the inclusion of all existing texts in the Docuverse might appear attractive, there is good reason to suggest that a limited subset might satisfy the requirements of many readers in certain disciplines and subject areas. This follows from the fact that much scientific and technical information has a limited 'shelf life', after which its importance gradually declines. The demand for scientific journal information clearly demonstrates this factor. The ADONIS project was a full-scale evaluation study of the parallel publishing of bio-medical journals on paper and CD-ROM (see Campbell and Stern, 1987). A pilot study described by Clarke (1981) showed that, in the chosen subject area, readers were primarily interested in material less than three years old. Thus, for certain areas there may be little point in actually capturing archive material and this could effectively remove 100 year's production of books and journals from the 'electronic queue' for well established disciplines. However, this is not to say that electronic bibliographic data should not be available.

Electronic versions

It is now standard practice for printed text to be processed electronically at some stage, although there is enormous variation in the precise form which such processing takes. Many authors create documents on word processors or microcomputers. An increasing number of publishers are prepared to accept electronic versions of texts or camera-ready copy instead of manuscripts or typed drafts, and the majority of publishers/printers produce a final electronic version as input for a typesetting machine. Thus, for the majority of texts published today, an electronic version of some kind will have been created, from which a hypertext could be fashioned.

Many publishers claim to have tried accepting electronic versions of manuscripts from authors in the past but have abandoned the practice due to the

---

3 Alschuler (1989) gives a description of the problems encountered in the conversion of six conference papers into three hypertext formats — each conversion took two or three experts approximately two months; Collier (1987) describes the conversion of 17 pages of a printed text into Thoth-II format as taking 40 hours.

creation of an increased rather than decreased handling requirement. Frequently, the technical incompetence of authors and the difficulties in catering for a wide variety of disk formats and word processor file types are given as major problems. However, there has been a considerable degree of standardisation in the personal computer market in recent years with a few operating systems (i.e., MS-DOS and Apple Macintosh), disk formats (5¼" and 3½") and word processor packages (MS-Word, Word Perfect) in a dominant position. In addition, virtually every current word processor is capable of generating files in the industry standard ASCII format.

The nature of the transformation

There are sound reasons for suggesting that the content and structure of many documents may be largely maintained following conversion from text to hypertext, and preservation of these aspects would certainly reduce the labour costs of the conversion. There are many types of text which have a strongly regulated content, and conversion to electronic format would be no reason to make amendments. Examples include industrial standards, guidelines, codes of practice, legal documents, technical documentation, historical records and religious documents.

In terms of a text's structure, alterations can obviously vary from merely rearranging the sequence of the original macro-units (sections/chapters) to completely reorganising the material into a new structure (hierarchy, flat alphabetical sequence or net). Again, there are grounds for suggesting that some texts may be converted with relatively little restructuring. Some electronic texts such as computer operating system documentation (e.g., Symbolics' Genera) are published in parallel forms. There is an obvious need for both forms to have equivalent contents, but there is also a considerable advantage in maintaining a consistency of structure for the reader. Such readers may have gained considerable knowledge of the structure of the pre-existing printed version and may be confused by a radically different electronic structure. Users may also need to use both versions as the situation demands, and this could be under conditions of extreme stress. Consider, for example, operating procedures for an industrial plant which are normally accessed electronically but which also exist as a printed document in case of a total power failure. Many recent technical texts have benefitted from the increased importance of document design as an area of professional activity and are consequently well structured with regard to the users' requirements.

Text mark-up

Recent advances in electronic text processing — and in particular the use of text mark-up — represents another form of assistance to the creation of hypertexts. In its broadest sense 'mark-up' refers to any method used to distinguish equivalent units of text such as words, sentences or paragraphs, or of indicating the various structural features of text such as headings, quotations, references or abstracts. Thus, the use of inter-word spacing, punctuation, indentation and contrasting typefaces are also examples of mark-up. However, mark-up is conventionally divided into two classes depending on whether it is *procedural* or *descriptive*.

Procedural mark-up, such as the Unix 'nroff' and 'troff' systems, refers to the special control characters that are inserted into electronic text files prior to their submission and subsequent interpretation by output devices such as photo-typesetting machines. Different codes are attached to section headings, paragraphs of body text, references and even individual characters and words so that each is set in an appropriate type style, size and line spacing. For example, to achieve the following emboldening:

"Answer question two **or** three."

the following troff mark-up would be necessary

"Answer question two \fB or \fR three."

The first command (\fB) instructs the typesetting machine to print the following characters in Times Bold. The second instruction (\fR) tells the output device to revert to the default style — Times Roman.

Descriptive mark-up further separates the description of the document from the interpretation by any particular output system since an item of descriptive mark-up is simply a label or 'tag' which is attached to a paragraph of body text or a chapter heading. Since no directions about formatting are included, the interpretation of the mark-up tags occurs entirely within the output system. This approach allows for greater flexibility in terms of moving text files between different mark-up and output systems. A generic descriptive markup system called Standard Generalised Mark-up Language (SGML) has been accepted as an ISO standard (ISO 8879) and is likely to become even more widely used in the future. (For an introduction to SGML, see Holloway, 1987.)

The generic coding of the structural units of documents via SGML, or some similar system, is likely to be of considerable significance to the future development of hypertext. It would enable the automatic generation of basic hypertexts which are based on document structure (i.e., the creation of nested hierarchies and the direct linkage of text elements) with a minimum of human involvement. Niblett and van Hoff (1989) describe a program (TOLK) that allows the user to covert SGML documents into a variety of hypertext and text forms for display or printing. Rahtz, Carr and Hall (1990) describe a hypertext interface

(LACE) for electronic documents prepared using L^AT_EX.

Perhaps of greater significance is the US Department of Defence Computer-aided Acquisition and Logistic Support (CALS) programme. CALS has the aim of converting all the significant documentation supporting defence systems from paper to electronic forms via internationally agreed standards, including SGML. Although CALS will initially concern only the armed forces and their contractors, the size of the defence 'industry' in America means the programme will soon have a major impact far beyond this sector.

The creation of original hypertexts

Although there may be grounds for suggesting that the conversion of printed documents to hypertext format may not be as daunting as it initially appears, this issue is seen as comparatively trivial by many proponents of hypertext. This is because conversion in this fashion does not attempt to alter the logical structure of the text — the arrangement of paragraphs or sections within sequential chapters is largely maintained, even if accessing and manipulating them is very different. Writing directly in hypertext enables completely new text structures to be considered by the author, and the design problems raised by these possibilities are generally seen as the main issues in the creation of hypertext.

The design of any non-fiction text can be seen as reflecting the interaction of tool (i.e., text), task and user (as discussed in Chapter 3) and contemporary readers are sophisticated enough to readily accept a whole range of text types. A telephone directory, car repair manual and college textbook are clearly all 'books' although they are designed to suit very different requirements. This acceptance is only realised individually after many years of experience in using books, and is also the product of a cultural experience with books stretching back hundreds of years (as discussed in Chapter 2). It involves a set of expectations and skills, cognitive and manipulative, which are associated with some of the most basic conventions of book design. These conventions (e.g., contents list at the front, index at the back, and binding down the side rather than at the top of the page) are rarely violated by the designer and permit a skilled reader to approach almost any book and use it with confidence. This situation contrasts sharply with the unique organisational structures and interfaces of hypertext systems.

The various hypertext systems currently available reflect the demands of a wide range of domains and potential tasks and it is important to bear in mind the notion of 'horses for courses' when considering whether a particular hypertext system is appropriate for a given application. Computer supported systems such as hypertext are never likely to attain the level of commonality that is characteristic of books.

Printing has been a relatively stable technology for 500 years; computing is not only new and rapidly evolving, but one of its characteristic features is the separation of information from storage medium. Computer text has no set physical shape — computers create virtual worlds. However, this is not to say that every hypertext system need, or should, be unique. A well designed hypertext system will not only embody principles of good user interface design but will also recognise the models that users are likely to bring to the system — models which may well be based on experience with print technology, as we discussed in Chapter 4.

Marchionini and Shneiderman (1988) recognised the breadth of strategies that could be supported by hypertext systems, from semi-directed browsing to systematic, iterative strategies using Boolean operators and a thesaurus of terms. They optimistically propose that the solution is to build "flexible, powerful human-computer interfaces to maximise benefits for every community of users." This seems in conflict with the received wisdom of system design (which they also reiterate) — successful system usage depends on the mental model that the user has for the system and this in turn is dependent on the conceptual model that the designer offers for the system (Norman, 1986). A flexible conceptual model proposed by the designer is unlikely to translate into clear system models for the users. This danger is recognised by Trigg and Irish (1987) who suggest that a sprawling and incoherent system is likely to be the result of attempting to cater for the broad spectrum of writing styles.

A standardised hypertext system seems a forlorn hope simply as a result of the variety of tasks to which hypertext can be applied.[4] In addition there is good reason to suggest that radically different systems may be appropriate for presenting, as opposed to creating, a given hypertext. By way of example we will consider a single text type — the extended, expository prose style of essays, journal articles and monographs. While many of the issues are relevant to other text types (course texts, technical documentation, encyclopædia, and so forth), the extended argument is not only central to higher education but is probably the 'model' that most frequently comes to mind as an example of a non-fiction form.

The characteristics of extended prose arguments

While the details vary considerably, a common structural model for the extended essay is taught in schools and colleges and is subsequently used by writers and expected by readers. The complete text comprises a limited number of arguments

---

4   The range is greater than that covered by text applications since other media (e.g., sound, image and video) can be incorporated.

(chapters/sections). Each of these is composed of various sub-elements (paragraphs) which may correspond to individual ideas/assertions or pieces of supporting evidence. The text will often have an introduction which summarises the arguments, the material to be covered and may also indicate the significance of the argument and its relation to other texts. This is followed by a presentation of the main arguments in detail - the *proof* in classical rhetoric. Finally, there will probably be a conclusion which reiterates the main points of the analysis and possibly suggests some solution to the 'problem' being addressed.

Two features of the model are of particular relevance to hypertext. First, this model appears to employ a distinctly linear structure, with each section developing the argument created by those preceding, albeit with internal references and repetition. Secondly, this model assumes that the evidence presented will be strictly selected and interpreted according to the needs of the argument. If this model underlies the creation and subsequent usage of 'scholarly' texts, what are the implications of writing in hypertext for this document type? The question occurs to most hypertext researchers: 'Is this conventional model a limitation that hypertext can help overcome by allowing an increased amount of supportive evidence and, more importantly, multiple interpretations?'

It is frequently argued that print technology is too rigid in the way that it enables information to be presented since a book presents the same facts in the same order to every reader irrespective of their current understanding or task requirements. This claim is patently true but only in a very limited sense since, as we saw in Chapter 2 and contrary to conventional wisdom, the physical linearity of printed texts is rarely a determinant of the way in which they are used. Access mechanisms (word spacing, typographical design, layout, indices, etc.) and their associated reading skills have evolved to overcome the constraints imposed by the fixed format of printed texts. In addition, the characteristics of individual readers — their interests, motivations and reading abilities — interact in such a fashion that although they may all read the same document, every reader will derive different information from it. Nevertheless, it is argued that with a hypertext network, readers are empowered to choose from a variety of different ways of viewing the information and the author is 'freed' from the convention (or requirement) of presenting only a single interpretation of the facts.

The hypertext network or 'web of facts'

Advocates of hypertext suggest that the ideas relevant to a subject can be represented best by a simple associative network, or web, with multiple inter-relationships specified. Electronic storage and manipulation makes it feasible to have a very large amount of material included and the hypertext format 'frees' the content from being structured with a specific ordering. According to Beeman *et al.* (1987), "a hypertext should function like an adventure game, permitting you to wander through a world of facts and ideas, jumping from one to another or linking them when you wish to do so." This vision transfers the responsibility for structuring the information away from the author and vests it jointly, if not equally, with the reader.

Streitz (1990) advocates flexible hypertext formats over conventional paper based formats for representing knowledge. He suggests that hypertexts can actually represent the author's 'internal knowledge structure' which can then be directly apprehended by the reader without the need for an intermediate stage, i.e., the traditional paper document with its apparently linear structure.[5] The idea is also proposed by Baird and Percival (1989) who claim that "information can be put into the hypertext in the same structure as it is in the author's head."

For Jonassen (1990) hypertext is eminently appropriate because "hypertext mimics the associative networks of human memory", a notion derived directly from Vannevar Bush's seminal paper in 1945 and subsequently repeated (often uncritically) by many commentators. Bush recognised the constraints of traditional alphabetic indexing and claimed that:

> "The human mind does not work that way. It operates by association. With one item in its grasp, it snaps instantly to the next that it is suggested by the association of thoughts, in accordance with some intricate web of trails carried by the cells of the brain."

Thus, a model of the way the brain stores information is proposed as an appropriate model for structuring and presenting information.[6] While Bush accepted that an artificial duplication of this mental process was unrealistic, he nevertheless suggested that it should be possible to at least emulate it. As we mentioned in Chapter 1, Bush proposed an information storage and retrieval system, called the memex, which would support 'associative indexing', "the basic idea of which is a provision whereby any item may be caused at will to select immediately and automatically another."

The perspective outlined by Bush is congruent with contemporary theories of memory which have arisen with the emergence of the computer in the 1960s, and

---

5   The existence of pre-written structured knowledge seems optimistic; most writers would surely agree with Aldous Huxley that ideas come in 'driblets' which have to be repeatedly re-written before anything coherent is achieved.

6   The inter-relationship of memory and understanding is virtually inevitable since we cannot understand something if we cannot remember it, although *not* necessarily vice versa — see Bartlett (1932).

this results in a curious paradox. Those commentators who suggest that associative networks are an appropriate model for the structure of electronic hypertexts are in fact alluding to a psychological perspective — man as an information processing system — which was itself strongly influenced by models of computer architecture.[7] However, even a brief review of the concept of association within human memory indicates that the parallel is facile.

Associationism has been a cornerstone of our view of memory and conceptual understanding for a very long time. It was a key element for the British empirical philosophers of the 16th century (Locke, Hume, Berkeley, James Mill and John Stuart Mill) and was also central to much of the work of the learning theorists who dominated experimental psychology in the first half of this century. The central concept is very simple: when two elements are experienced as occurring together in time (contiguously) they will become associated in memory.[8] Recent models of semantic memory have had a strong associative component and have even been described as being "neo-associationist" (Anderson and Bower, 1973). In these models, long-term memory is depicted as a 'network' of countless associations between verbal and conceptual entities, and memory retrieval becomes a search through this maze of pathways.

However, such theories differ radically from the original associationist views in terms of complexity. A variety of new features have been incorporated and these include logical relations between elements, hierarchical structures, and a new stress on context and strategy (see, for example, Collins and Quillian, 1969; Anderson and Bower, 1973; Collins and Loftus, 1975; Rumelhart and Ortony, 1977; Norman, Gentner and Stevens, 1976).

Of primary importance has been the incorporation of subordinate and superordinate relations between semantic categories (Collins and Quillian, 1969), since this led to the inclusion of logical inference in models of memory. Figure 11 depicts a simple but plausible semantic network centred on the concept *bitter* in which length of line is negatively correlated with strength of association, i.e., the shorter the line, the stronger the association. A number of limitations are clearly illustrated by even a cursory examination. The associations indicated are arbitrary, and many other linkages between the terms represented could easily be justified; the concepts are at different levels of generality, e.g., the inclusion of the concepts *aperitif, wine* and *sherry*; the concept depicted is relatively simple and easily

---

7   While this results in high levels of apparent consistency there is a danger that the explanation may become circular and the discussion divorced from a lower level of explanation. It should be remembered that very little is understood concerning the physical basis of memory while the physical storage of computer information is well understood.

8   This is one of the very few things which is not only a commonplace of everyday experience but has also been confirmed in countless experiments in psychology.

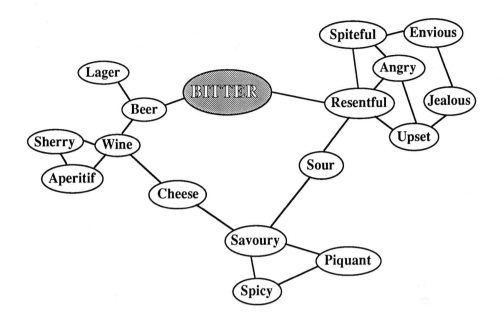

Figure 11: A simple associative semantic net for the concept *bitter*. [After Collins and Loftus, 1975]

defined but many others are much more ambiguous and likely to entail almost unlimited association, at which point graphical representation acts to reduce clarity rather than aid understanding. Finally, while there may be areas of significant agreement between individuals, ultimately semantic nets are unique to the individual.

A more sophisticated attempt at representing human memory is shown in Figure 12 where, although concepts are still linked by association, the linkages comprise specific types.[9] The graphic representation for even this simple factual episode is reasonably complex and it seems doubtful whether the approach is suitable for representing anything more involved. The Thoth-II system (Collier, 1987) attempts to do this by employing conceptual objects and typed relations, but the author accepts that there are substantial disadvantages to the approach, particularly with regard to user navigation. It is unclear at present how this structuring can be presented to the user in a way that is *meaningful*, let alone *helpful*.

---

9   The historical event is represented as a sequence of actions and the 'grammar' is initially confusing since it does not conform to the subject-verb-object (SVO) ordering expected by English speakers.

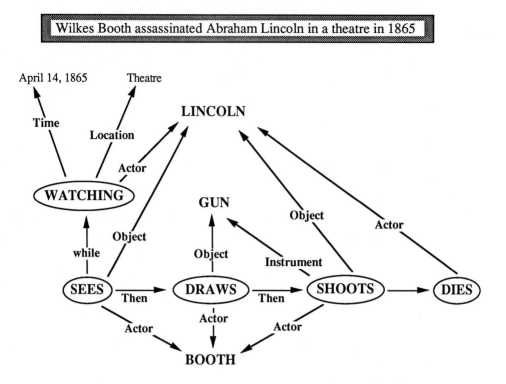

Figure 12: Semantic network for a simple historical episode. [After Rumelhart, Lindsay and Norman, 1972]

Our theoretical understanding has come a long way from the simple notions of the Associationists, but even the relatively sophisticated contemporary models of semantic memory and conceptual understanding are acknowledged to be crude representations. The claim that a simple, non-hierarchical associative net, or web, is an ideal or natural model for hypertext because it mimics human memory must be seen as inadequate.

The fallacy of simple networks as 'ideal' representations of knowledge

Although the extensive, unstructured or semi-structured net has gained popular approval as a generic model for hypertext systems, it has also been found seriously deficient. Both the lack of structure and the importance of very large data sets have been criticised. Whalley (1990) claims that arbitrary webs of facts can have no semantic significance since they are likely to be devoid of context and relevance to the individual reader and are nowhere near the same level of complexity as human knowledge structures. He neatly describes the limitations:

> "The hypertext reader might flit about between the trees with greater ease and yet still not perceive the shape of the wood any better than before."

Duffy and Knuth (1990) address a similar point when they suggest that the essentially exploratory type of reading which a net hypertext elicits denies the importance of goals and/or tasks. Reading, like any other information seeking activity, is purposeful: students read texts to pass exams or write essays; technicians read documentation to solve problems, and so on. Few writers aim merely to transfer a body of factual information to the reader, even if the local semantic connections are made explicit.[10] The level of analysis or conceptualisation is simply too low. Thus, Duffy and Knuth suggest in a learning context that "simply learning the links in a database is certainly not going to result in someone thinking like the professor."

An aspect of hypertext systems that is often proposed as an advantage is their potential for supporting very large bodies of information. However, Bereiter and Scardamalia (1987) contrast skilled and unskilled (or novice) writers and differentiate between the associated story re-telling and story transforming abilities. Similarly, teaching and learning in the broadest sense are concerned with the transmission of knowledge not simply the transfer of relatively unstructured information — we may *know* facts but we *understand* theories and perspectives. The creation of very large hypertext systems may be of limited value unless they are structured in such a way as to be coherent to the reader.

While a reader might spend considerable amounts of time 'browsing' paper documents, this activity is rarely haphazard.[11] Browsing is the process by which scanned material is evaluated for relevance according to a set of needs or interests (which may be capable of only vague definition by the reader), with irrelevant material being quickly rejected. This activity is enabled by the conventions of text layout and typography. A skilled reader need often only swiftly glance at the headings/sub-headings and opening paragraph in order to gain a good impression of the scope of a document.[12]

However, it is not clear that this type of information-seeking can be supported

---

[10] The aversion to 'structure' implied by proponents of hypertext webs seems to echo the impoverished approach to education propounded by Charles Dickens in *Hard Times*. Thomas Gradgrind, a Utilitarian school teacher, starts the novel with the following words: "Now, what I want is, Facts. Teach these boys and girls nothing but Facts. Facts alone are wanted in life."

[11] The patient in the dentist's waiting room may feel that his reading is totally aimless but it is still selective.

[12] This facility is most fully developed in the broadsheet style of newspaper.

by hypertext systems that entail relatively flat semantic networks or by computer systems which use small sized displays that are undifferentiated typographically. Richardson, Dillon and McKnight (1989) carried out an experimental study in which subjects used either a small or large computer display to search for items of information in a text. While no difference was found in terms of success, a clear preference was shown for the larger display. Of more significance was the finding that, even allowing for the fact that the small display showed less text, the text was manipulated significantly more in the small display condition than in the large display condition. This suggest that the readers' browsing may have been hampered by the small amount of text displayed at any one time.

The problem of adequately supporting browsing has been recognised in the design of some hypertext systems. For example, KMS has a pronounced hierarchical structure and rapid system response which are designed to support browsing. The consistent structure within and across hypertexts help orient the reader and the overview nature of the frames provides expectancies about what an unread section is likely to contain (in terms of content breadth and depth). Although there has been little experimental investigation of the potential advantages of various hypertext structures, there is evidence to support the adoption of hierarchical structures.

For example, Simpson and McKnight (1990) report an experiment in which subjects were provided with a range of structural cues to support them in accessing a hypertext: an alphabetical index; hierarchical contents list; typographical cues and current position indicator.[13] The hierarchical contents list was associated with more efficient navigation through the document and subsequent location of information. In addition, maps produced of the hypertext structure were more accurate for subjects who had had the hierarchical cues.

However, if simple hypertext webs are not appropriate vehicles for teaching or learning (transmission of knowledge) they may have an important rôle in the preparation of conventionally structured texts.

From chaos to order, from order to understanding?

Traditionally, scholarly writing has been concerned with the "transformation of inchoate ideas into coherent structures" (Smith, Weiss and Ferguson, 1987). Although there is no universally accepted model of the writing process, there *is* general agreement over the components of the main stages. Figure 13 represents

---

[13] With any study of this type there are always problems concerning the inherent structure of the text — some texts convert to hierarchical hypertexts more successfully than others.

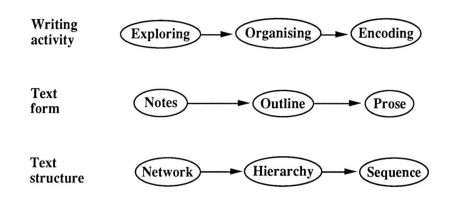

Figure 13: The stages in the production of conventional 'linear' text. [After Rada *et al.*, 1989]

these stages in terms of the author's activities, the external form of the text and the underlying logical structure. We will briefly sketch out the author's tasks and then see how hypertext may support them.

Initially, there must be some spur to undertake the work, be it intellectual (an alternate explanation for a body of facts or a resolution to an apparent theoretical inconsistency) or simply financial (a better mousetrap!) At this stage the 'text' will comprise at the very least a vaguely thought out theme and some supporting ideas which may be realised as an outline for approval by a publisher. Likely areas for initial investigation, such as relevant journals or individual authors, may also be known. From this beginning, three successive phases in the production of a text can be identified: exploration, organisation, and writing.

Exploration

This stage is concerned with general knowledge acquisition or 'fact finding', and involves searching citation indices and abstract journals and all the other activities which are relevant to a literature search. The process may seem disorderly since multiple avenues may be followed in parallel, and relevance thresholds may be initially set quite low. In addition, semantic associations within the information may be missing or erroneous. In order to manage the rapidly expanding collection of references, notes, quotations and photocopies, many authors resort to systems based on the card index file which provide an external memory without imposing any particular semantic structure (linear or otherwise) on the data.

Organisation

There is a gradual shift in emphasis away from fact finding and towards orienting, structuring and then re-structuring the growing body of material. This will involve examining the data from different theoretical perspectives and making inferences and deductions. These processes indicate gaps in the knowledge base which prompt further information seeking in an iterative fashion. Hierarchical structures will begin to take shape as superordinate/subordinate relations are perceived (or imposed) and sequences of cause and effect are established.

Writing

Smith, Weiss and Ferguson (1987) see this final stage as the culmination of a transition from what is essentially an information network to a hierarchy of concepts and relations. This phase initially involves the selection and arrangement of the knowledge generated during the first two stages to meet the author's rhetorical, or discourse, goals. The author will often have to choose between a number of pieces of supporting evidence for the sake of clarifying the argument. This is followed by a cycle of drafting, editing and revising at a much finer level of detail.

Word processing has significantly assisted this process through the ease with which revisions can be made to a text at all stages in the life cycle, but has barely improved on the initial data collection and organisation. Many authors still prefer to use file cards because of the ease of searching and, more importantly, sorting the notes. These requirements can be easily and effectively catered for by using a network-based hypertext system. Individual notes and references can be created as nodes in the network and then repeatedly grouped and regrouped as often as required. Mini-hierarchies, groupings, classifications and so forth can be assembled and discarded without abandoning serious investments of time and effort.

Trigg and Irish (1987) describe the experiences of 20 authors when using NoteCards, a sophisticated network-based hypertext system, to help in the preparation of a variety of texts. NoteCards was found to be particularly appropriate when the task was considered complex and likely to require major reorganisation rather than simply editing or revision. They identified an overhead concerning the effort required to input the information, which tends to reduce the attraction of using NoteCards for shorter or less complex texts.

If NoteCards-like systems can be useful aids in the preparation of conventional hierarchical texts, it is less clear that they can help in the presentation of those texts to readers. Experimental evidence from the field of document design suggests that "readers understand and learn more easily from texts when the information is set out in well defined structures and when the text provides clear signals of shifts from one part to another" (Charney, 1987). Thus, guidelines for technical prose (e.g., Kieras, 1985; Hartley, 1978) recommend that texts should be organized hierarchically and that this structure should be supported by the typographic layout; general comments should precede specific information; and presuppositions and transitions between sections should be made explicit.

Probably the strongest support for the importance of hierarchical structuring in the comprehension of expository or technical text comes from the experimental and theoretical work on reading undertaken in the fields of text processing and discourse analysis (see, Kintsch, 1974; Meyer, 1975; Kintsch and van Dijk, 1978). In summary, the widely accepted theory of text comprehension proposes that readers maintain two representations of the text. The first is a verbatim representation of successive text fragments which are held temporarily (i.e., in *short term memory*). The second is called the *textbase* and is a hierarchical semantic structure extracted from the contents of the initial, or surface, representation.

Comprehension is assumed to be an essentially 'bottom-up' process in which successive fragments are formed into the basic building blocks of the textbase. These semantic units are called micropropositions and, in total, they comprise the text's microstructure. Through the action of various rules of combination and reduction, this microstructure is successively reduced in an iterative fashion to produce higher order macropropositions and the text's macrostructure. The higher order macropropositions define the 'gist' of the argument contained in the text and are typically reproduced in readers' summaries. Following criticism of earlier versions of this theory van Dijk and Kintsch (1983) extended it to include a *situational* model. This refinement allowed for the continuous application of domain specific knowledge from long term memory for the construction of the macrostructure (i.e., the process is recognised as also containing 'top-down' components).

Conclusion

Given the dominant model of the comprehension process and the practical guidance commonly addressed to technical authors, it seems a brave stance to advocate an underlying model for hypertext which is anything other than hierarchical — at the document level at least. This approach has been adopted in very different ways by KMS and Guide, but their success remains open to evaluation.

Particularly in the case of the style of extended prose we have considered here, the author's task would seem to be to *simplify* the argument in order that it can be more easily grasped. This simplifying process involves the imposition of structure on a set of facts, opinions or arguments. The author who fails to simplify and who merely presents a collection of randomly[14] linked chunks of information will not be well-understood.

---

14 It will appear random to the reader even if the author considered them purposeful, for precisely the reason that the author has failed to make the purpose clear. The reader's task can be considered to be the extraction of the 'signal' from the background 'noise', and the poor author is one who fails to make the signal stand out.

CHAPTER SIX

HYPERTEXT, LEARNING AND EDUCATION

"When I think back on all the crap I learned in High School, it's a wonder I can think at all."

Paul Simon: Kodachrome®

Introduction

Since many people have seen hypertext as a replacement for printed information, it is not unnatural to suppose that it might have an impact in the field of education. After all, a vast number of printed texts are aimed specifically at the educational market, from the primary level to the tertiary level and beyond. A recent NATO Advanced Research Workshop was devoted to the design of hypertext for learning (Jonassen and Mandl, 1990), presumably based on the assumption that hypertext does have a real contribution to make. Indeed as we shall see below, it has been suggested that hypertext not only offers different information presentation techniques but also fosters a particular (and desirable) style of thinking.

Arguably, education is the most important activity in which civilised societies engage, and hence anything which claims to impact this process at such a fundamental level as the style of thinking which an individual uses must be taken seriously. In this chapter we will examine the potential of hypertext in educational environments and assess the work already conducted in this area. However, in order to provide a perspective on why hypertext might have any contribution to make, we will consider the rôle of the computer (or rather, the microcomputer) in education and in so doing, consider the nature of education itself.

In the early psychological literature, learning was often equated with memory, the recall of items in a list and so forth. However, the predominant view within the education system is that *real* learning, the kind the education system is about, goes beyond simple memory, as the following quote from Kelly (1984) serves to illustrate:

> "...education in the full sense goes some way beyond the mere acquisition of knowledge or of certain skills, that essentially it is a process which is concerned with some kind of personal development which is the result of the acquisition of this knowledge and those skills, and that this development is of a moral, social and emotional kind and is not restricted to the intellectual. Such a process will therefore involve the growth of understanding as well as the acquisition of knowledge, it will include the development of a system of values as well as of a cognitive perspective, and it will entail, as a corollary of all this, the ability to make a continuing critical review of one's knowledge, one's understanding and one's moral and social values." (p. 8-9)

In Western countries at least, society sees fit to provide not only an educational environment (schools, colleges, and so forth) but also to provide learners with some final statement of their achievements in that environment, to offer a 'critical review' based on the teacher's view of what the learner has achieved. Such statements could in principle take the form of a description of the experiences to which the learner had been subjected (e.g., courses in history, geography, mathematics) in the way in which articles of apprenticeship used to be written. However, other societal pressures (e.g., limited availability of work) have led to the statements taking the form of marks gained in an examination. Hence, the examination is the educational system's response to the problem of measuring the understanding which the learner has achieved.

Understanding or comprehension is also the concern of many psychologists, as we have discussed in previous chapters. However, as educationalists are quick to point out, translating psychological theory into educational practice is not easy and, in many cases, of questionable desirability. For example, the 'programmed learning' techniques which Skinner developed from his theories of animal learning were enthusiastically adopted by many but have now largely fallen into disuse. Theorists such as Skinner were not concerned with abstract terms like comprehension, preferring to stick with observable behaviour. Such a stance provides for easy evaluation but does not accord with broader views of learning and education. Even theorists who have explicitly attempted to elucidate the concept of comprehension have failed to produce anything which the average teacher could make use of. For example, consider the work of van Dijk and Kintsch (1983). As we mentioned briefly in Chapters 3 and 5, they see knowledge as consisting of propositions and hence any discourse (written or spoken) will contain propositions and implied or explicit relationships between them. These propositions can be combined into higher-level propositions, or macropropositions. In effect, then, someone who reads a text and writes a summary or extracts the 'gist' can be viewed as extracting the macropropositions from that text.

The methods derived by van Dijk and Kintsch offer a means of analysing the propositional structure of text and thereby assessing comprehension by comparing the propositional structure of the original text with that produced by the reader. However, these methods are extremely long-winded and time consuming — aspects which are readily acknowledged by van Dijk and Kintsch in their 1983 book which describes the techniques in detail. Such methods may have a sound basis in psychological theory, and indeed the present authors have used them successfully (albeit with some difficulty) to assess readers' comprehension of journal articles (Richardson, McKnight, Dillon and Forrester, 1989). However, it would not be feasible to transfer such techniques to the school-room. It could be argued that teachers are performing a sort of informal propositional analysis when they read and mark an essay, but it is precisely this informality which educational evaluators argue against.

No matter how they are derived, examination marks or course grades are also used as a method of assessing the effectiveness of teachers and educational material. Hence, many studies have compared two groups of learners, one of whom used some new educational material, in an attempt to evaluate the material. Of course some yardstick is necessary to judge educational material against; without any evaluation it is possible that material could be introduced which was detrimental to the learning process. As Borich and Jemelka (1981) say:

> "the purpose of evaluation is to provide decision makers with information about the effectiveness of an educational program, product or procedure."
> (p. 161).

However, it is difficult to reconcile the view of education described by Kelly above — a rich, personal development process — with the content and experience of examinations.

If learning is viewed as a personal process, the evaluation of learning ought to be related to the goals which the learner is trying to achieve. Indeed, some educationalists have espoused systems whereby each learner negotiates a 'personal learning contract' with a course tutor, conducts what they consider to be the appropriate work and then judges the outcome of the work against the aims stated in the contract. Although such schemes are typically described using terms like 'self-actualised learners', they essentially fall between two stools. On the one hand, if learners were truly self-actualised, why would they need a contract? Who is the contract with? On the other hand, unless it is believed that such schemes have obvious intuitive validity, they clearly require evaluation if they are to be widely promulgated. Furthermore, it has been suggested that the majority of students are not able to set learning objectives for themselves and study autonomously (Bunderson, 1974; O'Shea and Self, 1983).[1]

It is clear, then, that there are many different groups with a stake in the education system and it is perhaps ironic that the group with the biggest stake — the learners — have the least power. Rather than get further embroiled in the educational debate, and in order to advance the present discussion, let us accept that the aim of education is to encourage learning, and the effectiveness of education is somehow measured in terms of the learning which takes place. How, then, might the process of learning be encouraged? Again, a quote from Kelly (1984) serves to illustrate a commonly held view within the educational system:

> "Such a process is best forwarded, therefore, not by teaching of a straight didactic kind, which can so readily and so often lead to the acquisition of knowledge of a kind which in no sense becomes fully a part of one's being or has any impact on one's view of life...it can only be promoted by forms of learning in which the mind of the learner is actively engaged, in which there is genuine interaction and interplay between the learner and the activities he is engaged in, in which those activities, in short, become genuine experiences to which a genuinely personal response is invited and encouraged. This in turn suggests that any material we present to pupils must be relevant to them, encouraging them to see it as interesting for its own sake, must offer a challenge to their understanding, by confronting them with a problem to solve...must encourage them to ask their own questions rather than merely respond to ours...It is with the asking of questions rather than the learning of answers that true education begins." (p.9)

From this point of view, therefore, the best that a teacher or lecturer can do is to provide an environment in which the pupil can engage in the active cognitive processes necessary for learning; to act as a catalyst, a facilitator of the learning process rather than merely a provider of facts. What, then, might the microcomputer be able to contribute to this process?

If we were to look superficially at the typical use of the micro in primary schools, we might be forgiven for thinking that the computer was being used in a

---

1   We recognise the potentially circular argument here: students cannot set learning objectives or study autonomously because they have not been allowed to and therefore not developed such skills. To break out of the circle would require major changes to the educational system.

way antithetical to the sort of process described by Kelly above. In many instances, the software apparently presents little more than 'drill-and-practice' exercises which might easily be done on paper. However, even at the drill-and-practice level, it is possible to see advantages in the use of micros over traditional methods. Good software[2] will respond individually to each child, allow a change of pace to suit each child, provide instant feedback, enable the easy maintenance of pupil records and so forth. It is essentially an economic argument which puts a single teacher in charge of 20 – 30 children.[3] Potentially at least, the micro not only offers an opportunity for children to proceed at their own pace but also frees the teacher to identify and provide additional help for children in difficulty.

Argued at this surface level, then, even drill-and-practice software would seem to be advantageous to pupils. However, at a deeper level, critics of such software would argue that it merely reinforces a system of teaching which does little to advance true education. As Kutz (1985) puts it:

> "Precisely because this is simply a change of mechanism and little else, little is gained. In a setting where skills instruction predominates and drill is a primary means of that instruction, nothing of importance has changed. Children will still learn their multiplication facts and not know when to use them, will still learn lists of spelling words and not be willing or able to write a story, will still learn states and capitals and remain ignorant of both geography and history. It will look like the computer has made a difference in education but it will be, in the end, a rearrangement of the furniture." (p.20-21)

Kutz goes on to point out that it need not be so. He describes three programs which tackle such topics as graphing of mathematical functions, logic, note-taking and reasoning from information in ways which a teacher could not do using traditional methods. The *Green Globs* program (Dugdale, 1982) is a particularly good example. In this the screen shows 13 randomly placed 'green globs' in a coordinate system, the pupil types in an equation from an allowable class of equations, the computer plots the graph of the equation, and any globs through which the graph passes explode and increase the pupil's score. The scoring rewards hitting many globs with one curve, so the pupil is encouraged to consider carefully the choice of equation. While such topics have been taught for many years,

---

2   We must assume in what follows that software is well-written, with clear educational objectives embodied in it. Unfortunately, in many cases, schools use software which does not measure up to such criteria. However, since they may also use badly written text-books, we make our assumption in order to consider the *potential* of micros in education.

3   If evidence is required to support this statement, consider the closing of many rural schools in Britain and the subsequent 'bussing' of children.

programs like this enable qualitative changes in the learning process to occur; the tedium of calculation and plotting of the graph with anything but simple coefficients is removed, allowing the pupil to get rapid feedback about the effect of changes in the equation chosen.

Kutz omits to mention that all three of his examples present educational material in the context of a game, and it could be argued that such a context 'trivialises' the material. However, it could equally be argued that such a context readily promotes the active engagement espoused by Kelly above. Furthermore, if we accept that a complex process such as education might involve various sub-processes or tasks, then it is not unreasonable to suggest that some of these tasks may be amenable to drill-and-practice while others might not. It then becomes a matter of judgement when to use the various types of software.

If we accept, then, that the microcomputer is a tool which, like many other tools, might be used to advantage in an educational setting, the question arises of how we can assess the effectiveness of the micro in education. As we saw earlier, the question of assessing comprehension or understanding is not one to which an unequivocal answer can be given. Seymour Papert (1980) — arguably the most influential figure in the field of computers in education, and the developer of the LOGO language — suggests that programming and functioning within computer-controlled microworlds will influence a learner's cognitive style and understanding of some of the most powerful ideas in science and mathematics, but he also cautions that such changes should not be judged by whether the changes produce a measurable improvement in traditional course performance. In Papert's view, it is possible that both the mechanics and the purpose of education will need to change before benefits become obvious.

The views of educationalists such as Papert and Kelly can be contrasted with those of O'Neil and Paris (1981) who, in arguing for the use of the term Computer-Based Instruction, say that 'instruction' can refer to either education or training. We saw above Kelly's description of education, from which point of view instruction and training refer to the acquisition of specific skills and are not to be confused with education. The evaluation of specific skills is marginally less controversial than the evaluation of educational practice, if only because many skills have clearly definable performance characteristics associated with them. To equate education and instruction is to make an error which a consideration of the etymology of the terms might help to avoid: 'instruction' derives from the Latin (*in* and *struere*) and means literally to pile *in*, whereas 'education' derives from the Latin (*e* or *ex* and *ducere*) and means to draw *out*.

Perhaps surprisingly, both views of education accept that the computer has a rôle to play. What differs is the precise nature of that rôle and therefore the method of evaluating its effectiveness. Within education, this difference in rôle has been characterised by the move away from the behaviourist approach typified by the linear, 'programmed learning' of Skinner (1968) towards the cognitive 'microworlds' or even the so-called 'intelligent tutoring systems'. However, as Duchastel (1988) has pointed out, much educational software presents information to the student in the same manner as a textbook.

We can see these disparate views of education as differing in terms of the task dimension described in Chapter 3. This is important when we turn to hypertext, because we must ask what task the user is trying to perform. Hypertext is a resource, like a book, and an information retrieval task may differ from, or form part of, a learning task. By concentrating on the task, we can consider the impact of hypertext on various components of the learning process and thereby provide a more accurate assessment of its utility. For example, it may be that hypertext better supports retrieval of specific, well-defined information, or it may better support the kind of browsing and 'getting a feel for an area' that is often required. To expect it to support all activities equally well would be unrealistic, as would the expectation that all instantiations of hypertext would offer equal support.

Of course, we could ask why we might expect hypertext to have anything special to offer. In answering this question, Barrett (1988) makes reference back to Papert, claiming that his ideas have relevance for designers of hypertext environments:

> "Hypertext systems can provide us with robust objects to think with: self-authoring texts that body forth the movements of a mind focused on a particular topic." (p.xix)

It is not clear what manner of thing a 'self-authoring text' is, and phrases like 'body forth the movements of a mind' have dubious meaning on several counts. However, on the basis that hypertext *has* been suggested as having a contribution to make to education, it becomes necessary to investigate the form that such a contribution could take.

As we said earlier, the evaluation of learning must be related to the goals or purposes with which the learning was undertaken. However, in a complex learning environment such as that offered by a hypermedia system, learning may take place which is unrelated to specific goals but which is nevertheless valuable. As Marchionini (1990) points out:

> "The essential problem of evaluating highly interactive systems is in measuring both the quality of the interaction as well as the product of

learning. Evaluations of hypermedia-based learning must address both the process of learning and the outcomes of learning." (p.20.6)

Evaluating learning in hypertext

Lineal versus non-lineal thinking

Beeman *et al.* (1987) offer a view of education very much in line with that outlined by Kelly above. They say that in the United States "higher education has traditionally been seen as contributing to an ongoing ontogenetic process. Through education the student is seen not only to acquire information, but also to develop new capacities as a human being." They see the goal of American and North European education as being to encourage the development of a 'non-lineal', pluralistic, relativistic or critical style of thinking. They contrast this with a 'lineal' style, which they identify particularly with the French and Japanese systems, in which "the basic function of education is then to exercise the brain through rote memorization and standard drill exercises with less attention to integration of that information."[4]

For Beeman *et al.*, the paradox of education is that it attempts to foster non-lineal thinking using lineal communication, presentation and instruction. They suggest that hypertext offers a solution to the paradox insofar as it can be used as an educational tool for promoting non-lineal thought, and their paper reports on attempts to use the Intermedia hypertext system in two of Brown University's existing courses — an English literature survey course and a plant cell biology course. The evaluation of the effect of introducing hypertext was far from easy. Each of the courses was closely observed by a team of social scientists, once prior to the introduction of hypertext and once when the hypertext materials were in use; instructors and students were interviewed several times throughout the evaluation; a group of students was asked to keep diaries of their activities during the time the courses were taught; and the use of a specially set up computer laboratory by both students and instructors was monitored.

At first sight, the effects of introducing hypertext seem to have been positive. Beeman *et al.* report a positive correlation ($r = 0.29$ at 0.05 level of confidence)[5]

---

4   It is difficult to reconcile Beeman's apparently derogatory view of French education with that country's undoubted contributions to, say, philosophy (from Descartes to Sartre). Furthermore, if the current Japanese domination of industry is a result of Japanese education, it is not surprising that some Western industrialists have argued for a reappraisal of Western education!

5   Although this correlation is statistically significant, it is worth remembering that the 'strength' of a correlation is best gauged by considering r^2. This value represents the proportion of the variance in Y accounted for by a knowledge of X. Hence a correlation of 0.29 means that less than 10%

between high Intermedia use and high grades. However, they also report an unexpected finding which suggests that improvements may not have been attributable to the introduction of hypertext *per se* but rather to factors related to its introduction. Because the Intermedia workstations were not ready in time, the professor in charge of the English course was forced to teach the course without using the system, but having already prepared the Intermedia material. The result of this was that he changed the way he taught the course and subsequently felt that students grasped pluralistic reasoning styles better than in previous years. Furthermore, the students were more satisfied with the course than in previous years. This suggests that the need to rethink the course design may have been the major contributor to the improvement in grades. A professor who has taught the same course for years may not be as 'inspiring' as he used to be, but interest may well be rekindled and communicated to the students by having to redesign the course for a new medium.

A further difficulty in making any strong statements about the apparent improvements in grades is also raised by Beeman. By themselves, the studies offer no evidence that the pluralistic thinking fostered in these two courses transfers to other courses. As Beeman points out, students are generally good at adapting to teachers because they are interested in doing well. Hence, their results may indicate a course-specific adaptation rather than a genuine change in thinking style. However, it would be extremely difficult to test such an hypothesis since it would involve the comparative evaluation of students across many courses.

The Beeman studies are an excellent illustration of the difficulties involved in assessing the effect of introducing not only hypertext but any new technique into a real-world setting. The well-known Hawthorne effect[6] is just as likely to appear in an educational setting. Furthermore, Beeman's most interesting conclusion was that the significant learning effects observed through the use of Intermedia were more pronounced for the people involved in *producing* the materials rather than students *using* the system, apparently substantiating the adage that 'the best way to learn about something is to teach it'!

Learning support environments
Despite the topic of learning having formed a major section of psychology for many years, we still know very little about the cognitive processes of learning.

---

of the variance in Y is accounted for by a knowledge of X.

6   The Hawthorne effect refers to the influence of the experimenter's presence, or the knowledge that one is taking part in an experiment, on subjects' behaviour. It is so named after its identification by social scientists at the Hawthorne Works of the Western Electrical Company in the 1920s.

Hence, evaluating the quality of the interaction, as recommended by Marchionini, is by no means straightforward, as he recognises. However, as Hammond (1989) points out, we seem to know a good deal about providing appropriate environments for learning:

> "This is the case both at an applied level and at the level of cognitive theory. For instance in 'teaching' a child to talk the parent merely needs to give appropriate stimulation at appropriate times; details of intermediate states of knowledge and the processes of acquisition can safely be left to the child and to the research psychologist." (p.172)

Hammond and Allinson (1989) suggest that hypertext can provide the basis for an exploratory learning system but that by itself it is insufficient, needing to be supplemented by more directed guidance and access mechanisms. In order to investigate this suggestion, they conducted an experiment in which all subjects used the same material held in a hypertext form, but with differing guidance and access facilities available. The baseline group had 'raw' hypertext with no additional facilities, while other groups had either a map or index or guided tours available, and a final group had all three facilities (map, index, tours) available. Half of the subjects were given a series of questions to answer while accessing the material (a directed task) while the other half were instructed to make use of the material to prepare for a subsequent multiple-choice test (an exploratory task).

Perhaps surprisingly, Hammond and Allinson report no reliable differences between task conditions for the three groups which had a single additional facility, although in all three groups the facilities were used to a substantial extent. However, in the group having all three facilities available there was a significant task-by-facility interaction. Those subjects performing the exploratory task made little use of the index but significant use of the tours, while those performing the directed task made little use of the tours and far more use of the index. Thus, Hammond and Allinson argue that after only 20 minutes subjects were able to employ the facilities in a task-directed manner.

The additional facilities also allowed more accurate overviews of the available material and resulted in a higher rate of exposure to new rather than repeated information. However, there were no significant differences in task performance between groups. Hammond and Allinson attribute this lack of difference to the fact that neither of the tasks required any strategic organisation of the material and they therefore caution against extrapolating such results to situations other than simple rote learning of relatively unstructured material. Indeed, even the subjective judgements of the subjects — that the system was easy to use, getting lost was not a major problem, and the system was rated as "better than a book" — should be viewed in the light of the fact that the hypertext used was very small (consisting of only 39 information screens) and subjects only used the system for a maximum of 20 minutes. Although it discusses 'learning support environments' and is clearly aimed at an educational context, Hammond and Allinson's work provides a contrast to the Beeman study in that its strength is its experimental rigour, whereas the strength of Beeman's work is its applied, 'real world' nature. Both types of study have a rôle to play in the attempt to discover the effects of hypertext in education.

Semantic nets and web learning

In Chapter 2 we discussed at length the notion that printed text is linear, in contrast to non-linear hypertext. As we pointed out, the notion of linear text is extremely pervasive but arguably misconceived. Nevertheless, Beeman is not alone in seeing a paradox between a fostering of non-linear thinking by using allegedly linear methods. According to Jonassen (1986), hypertext breaks what he terms the 'sequential processing tendency'. He claims to review "cognitive principles of learning that support the validity of hypertext designs for learning and information transfer", and what follows is a condensation of Jonassen's review.

Jonassen takes as his basis the statement by Norman (1976) that in order to be able to develop good tutorial teaching systems we need to be able to (a) represent subject matter knowledge and (b) model its structure, including knowledge representation, in a way that will (c) provide principles and strategies of instruction. The distinction Norman is making is between the (changing but generally accepted) state of knowledge about a subject and an individual's knowledge of that subject. Implicit in his argument is that if we can represent both of these states of knowledge in a manner in which they can be compared, then presumably the principles and strategies of instruction will be such as to move the individual's view closer to the general view.

Representation of subject knowledge

In order to design courseware consistent with knowledge representation, a method for representing knowledge is required. Jonassen points to semantic network models as the most universally accepted conception of knowledge. Such networks are comprised of nodes (which are instances of propositional structures) and links (which describe the propositional connection between the nodes). These networks may be used to describe both what a learner already knows and the information to be learned. From this point of view, learning involves acquiring new structures by constructing new nodes and interrelating them with each other and with existing nodes.

Modelling the structure of knowledge

Jonassen uses the notion of 'webs of information' as a convenient way of representing a learner's semantic network of concepts. Indeed, it is not clear how the concepts of 'web' and 'semantic net' differ since Jonassen says "learning is never complete, because the growth of the web (semantic network) never ceases completely" and one of his figures is labelled as a diagram "representing semantic network, that is, web of concepts to which new information could be integrated." He uses the concept of web to introduce so-called web learning principles as a means of meeting Norman's third requirement.

Web learning principles of instruction

According to such principles, the effective teacher presents material in a way that allows learners the opportunity to develop some framework for relating materials to each other (a web) and then elaborating the material. "According to web teaching principles, we should begin with a coarse web of information, outlining topics to be discussed and then giving a general overview, followed by detailed overviews, and finally detailed substructures."

For Jonassen, it is a short step from webs/semantic networks to hypertext. In order to avoid misrepresenting his position, we quote at some length:

> "Hypertext displays manifest web teaching methods. A good hypertext should begin by showing a map of the whole text such as in Figures 2, 3, and 6. This map represents the web of interrelated concepts contained in the hypertext.[7] An introductory set of screens would then lead into the hypertext which contains the detailed concepts. It would be easy to constrain the hypertext, requiring users to pass through the detailed overviews in order to get to the detailed substructure. These options are discussed in more detail in the implementation section.
>
> Fully applying web learning/teaching principles to instructional text or courseware goes a step further — matching the network structure of the subject matter with the semantic network of the learner. In doing so, the tutor
>
> 1. assesses knowledge of the learner and constructs a model of the knowledge
> 2. compares the knowledge of the student with the topic structure, noting gaps or inconsistencies

---

7   In fact, the figures are risible if they are seriously meant as representations of real-world hypertexts. As other authors have noted (e.g., Conklin, 1987), with a hypertext of any size it is simply not feasible to represent the structure of the entire contents in this way, but this is not to say that some organising principles are not necessary. For example, in the database of journal articles described in Chapter 7 it would be impossible to represent each node of knowledge and all the interconnections, but it is still necessary to organise the material and display the form which the organisation takes.

3. presents materials needed to fill the gaps; that is, presents new material based on the web teaching strategies

(Norman, 1976).

These procedures assume, of course, that we are able to adequately represent the structure of the subject matter as well as the semantic network of information possessed by the learner. Such instruction for large numbers of students would necessarily have to be computerized. Courseware, therefore, must provide the computer with a semantic network of knowledge about the topic and allow the learner to interact with it (Carbonell, 1970)."

Although the learner is allowed (*sic*) to interact with the knowledge, this view of learning is very much teacher-controlled. Assuming not only that the structure of both the learner's current knowledge and the topic can be represented but also that methods exist for making meaningful comparisons between such structures,[8] the aim is to "fill the gaps." This view seems at variance with Jonassen's statement earlier in the same article that learners should be allowed to determine what information is relevant to their needs as well as the sequence of presentation which is most meaningful to them.

More recently, Jonassen (1990) has attempted to use a variety of techniques such as multi-dimensional scaling in order to arrive at an expert view of a knowledge domain. The suggestion then is that such semantic networks can not only be seen as the expert's cognitive map but that such a map can provide the representation to be used as a graphical browser in a hypertext. There would certainly be good arguments for the graphical browser signalling the structure of the hypertext's contents to the reader, but it is not clear that this could be done at anything other than a gross level. It is certainly true that knowledge is multi-dimensional, so how much validity does a two-dimensional representation of that knowledge have? In fact, the same mathematical techniques which are used to dimensionalise the knowledge can often answer this question. For example, in the case of multi-dimensional scaling it is possible to associate a 'stress' value with each solution derived from the scaling data (Kruskal, 1964). Thus, if the stress associated with a four-dimensional solution is less than that associated with a three-dimensional solution, we can say that the former is a better fit to the data. It

---

8 Indeed, such assumptions are not completely unwarranted. Although based on Kelly's (1955) personal construct theory and repertory grid techniques rather than either semantic nets or webs, the work of Mendoza and Thomas (1972) can be seen to attempt exactly these representations, with comparisons being made in real time by a computer and reflected back to the learner. The reader interested in the connection between semantic networks and repertory grids is referred to Coltheart and Evans (1982).

follows, therefore, that for a two-dimensional solution to be used as the basis for a graphical browser, there would need to be an acceptably low stress level associated with it, otherwise the learner is being presented with an artificial overview. Hence, while the effort to provide really meaningful models of the information structure is to be applauded, care should be taken to ensure that such models have both mathematical and psychological validity.

Duffy and Knuth (1990) raise another problem relating to the use of an expert's view of a domain: which expert's view should be used? They elaborate this problem as follows:

"Is the project specific to a particular instructor's viewpoint? Would other faculty be willing to use this individual's representation? In essence...we would have to buy into a particular construction of knowledge. And if we wanted a generalizable product, then we would have to be sure that other instructors in the domain would buy into that construction as well."

Learner individuality

Stanton and Stammers (1990) suggest that the reasons why a non-linear environment is superior are that it (a) allows for different levels of prior knowledge, (b) encourages exploration, (c) enables subjects to see a sub-task as part of the whole task, and (d) allows subjects to adapt material to their own learning style. In their experiments (1989, 1990), one set of subjects was given the freedom to access a set of training modules in any order, while another set of subjects was presented with the modules in a fixed order. They reported that performance was significantly improved when subjects trained in the non-linear condition. Although such comparisons may provide valid experimental designs, extrapolating the results to realistic learning situations is difficult, particularly in higher education where students are rarely forced to access material in a rigid, predetermined order. Even at a primary school level, where it was once thought that number theory was a prerequisite for set theory, extrapolation is difficult. Hence, the results may reflect the advantage not so much of non-linear environments but rather of giving the learner some degree of control over the learning environment.

It could be argued that a hypertext environment does provide for greater learner control and therefore possesses advantages over traditional paper-based learning materials. Advocates of this view suggest that in a hypertext learners can go where they like, follow their own train of thought and so forth. However, this is patently not the case. Students using hypertext courseware will tend to follow the paths provided by the course tutor or hypertext author. In this case, hypertexts are more constraining than books which can be opened at any page. In principle, the whole of a book or journal volume is available to the reader simply by turning page after page,[9] whereas in hypertext the learner is at the mercy of the author, reliant on him having provided suitable links. Even if learners are given the facility to add their own links, they must have seen the nodes at both ends of the link in order to make the judgement that a link is desirable. This makes the process of adding links seem a little more 'hit-and-miss' than it is usually described.

Although the notion of control is an important one in education, it is far from clear that hypertext provides the learner with more control than traditional media. While Duchastel (1988) states that computers promote interaction through a manipulative style of learning where the student reacts to the information presented, the fact that the learner is using a mouse to select items and move through the information space does not make the process any more 'active' than consulting an index, turning the pages of a book, underlining passages and writing notes in the margin. In this sense, hypertext might be merely the latest in a long line of 'computer solutions' in education and any apparent benefits may be due to little more than novelty value.

Incidental learning

As we have said earlier, hypertext may well have something to offer for particular kinds of tasks. Marchionini and Shneiderman (1988), for example, have suggested that hypertext is more suited to browsing than directed retrieval tasks. Following from this suggestion, Jones (1989) hypothesised that more incidental learning[10] would occur in a browsing task than in a task requiring the use of an index. The argument advanced by Jones was that the links in a hypertext node represent an embedded menu and that the context provided by the node should encourage the connection of the ideas at either end of the link. In other words, the learner's semantic net is more likely to be elaborated or more learning is likely to occur.

Two groups of subjects were used in Jones's experiment. Both groups used the same hypertext database, but one group was shown how to browse through the information using the links and were explicitly instructed not to use the index, while the other group were instructed in the use of the index and were not informed about the active nature of the highlighted words on screen (which were

---

9   The importance of serendipitous finding of information is mentioned by several authors (e.g., Olsen, 1989). For example, how often have you noticed that the article which *follows* the one you're interested in is also interesting, despite having not retrieved it via the usual means? It is difficult not to design such findings out of hypertext, since any node will have a preset number of links when the learner reaches it. However, see the interface designed for the journal database described in Chapter 7.

10 Incidental learning is a well-documented phenomenon in the literature of psychology. It is the learning which occurs even though it may not be related to the goal of the learner (or even the teacher). Indeed, the game of Trivial Pursuit capitalises on the fact that we can often recall a wealth of 'facts' which we have never consciously learned or committed to memory.

described to them as 'clues to other index entries'). Subjects were given five questions to answer from the database, but afterwards were given 10 questions to measure incidental learning.

Although Jones's argument has intuitive appeal, her experiment failed to support her hypothesis. No significant differences were observed in terms of performance on the incidental learning questions. It is possible that the nature of the questions given to the subjects to answer from the database did not encourage incidental learning. This is certainly suggested by the low overall success level of subjects on the incidental learning test — the *highest* mean number correct for any group was 1.56. Even in the five target questions, taking all groups together, no question was answered correctly by more than half of the subjects. This suggests that the task was not particularly sensitive to the effect of the experimental manipulations and hence we can do little more than agree with Jones that "much more research is needed."

Does hypertext have a rôle to play in learning and education?

What, then, can we conclude on the basis of the foregoing? We have seen a variety of work ranging from the broad study by Beeman *et al* to the controlled experiments of Hammond and Allinson and Jones, and others exist in the literature which lie somewhere in between (e.g., Verreck and Lkoundi, 1990). However, none has demonstrated any appreciable advantage for hypertext. Like any of the new technologies brought into education — 'teaching machines' based on programmed learning, computer assisted learning, intelligent tutoring systems, even television — more claims have been made on hypertext's behalf than the experimental evidence has been able to support. It could be argued that strong claims need to be made about any innovative material in order for it to be taken seriously enough to be subjected to evaluation — in a fast-moving world, technologies which don't announce their presence with a loud shout tend to get ignored.

It would seem therefore that a degree of scepticism is not unwarranted where hypertext applications to learning are warranted, and we are not alone in suggesting this. Whalley (1990), for example, is openly critical of attempts to relate the webs of facts in a hypertext to human semantic knowledge structures, an exercise which he describes as "computer-science as epistemology and makes little sense"! However, rather than see hypertext as merely another flash in the educational pan, we would like to suggest that it *does* have a rôle to play within education and learning.

If we look at the intellectual activities of the majority of school, college and university learners, they involve the storage, retrieval and manipulation of information. Despite what educationalists say about personal development, self-actualisation, intrinsic motivation and all the other fine phrases, the fact is that students at all levels are presented with existing knowledge in a variety of forms (books, articles, lectures), they make notes on the information (either directly as marginalia or separately in notebooks), they reorganise the information for essays and so forth.

Hypertext offers a computer-based information environment which could support all these activities. It offers a framework for the storage, rapid retrieval and potentially easy manipulation of information (as we suggested in Chapter 5). Furthermore, it is also possible to integrate note-making and annotation facilities with 'given' texts (a requirement suggested strongly by the case studies reported by Leggett *et al.*, 1990). Such activities are fundamental to the process of education as it occurs in schools and colleges all over the world, and as such hypertext could provide a very valuable tool. We believe, as Megarry (1988) has suggested, that:

> "the rôle of the computer should be organizing and representing knowledge to give the user *easy access and control*, rather than trying to create a model of the learner and seeking to prescribe her route through it" (p.172, emphasis added).

In Britain, the new National Curriculum places special emphasis on the use of databases in all subjects, even at primary school level. The Domesday system was meant to be used by school children. It is a *large* database — 130,000 pages of text, 24,000 pictures and detailed maps of the British Isles on just one of the videodisks (the Community disk). Databases, and therefore potentially hypertext databases, are finding their way into schools, not just universities and colleges. The systems which children use in school are the systems they take for granted later in life. If hypertext is to have an impact on information retrieval and manipulation, it is worth considering the design issues relating to its use by school children as well as undergraduates.

Whether or not hypertext changes the way we think remains to be seen. Duffy and Knuth (1990) have argued convincingly that the promotion of non-linear thinking "rests primarily in the pedagogy of the professor rather than in the database." Their paper represents an excellent example of the requirement to consider the pedagogical principles on which the hypertext usage is to be based before considering the technology through which it will be instantiated, and it should be considered as required reading to all who would design hypertexts for use in learning and education.

CHAPTER SEVEN

THE HYPERTEXT DATABASE : A CASE STUDY

"He who can, does. He who cannot, teaches"
G.B. Shaw: Maxims for Revolutionists

In the preceding chapters we have attempted to present the various issues underpinning the emergence and use of hypertext, as well as highlighting the various application domains of this technology. In an attempt to demonstrate that much of this work has a practical basis in system development, and to embody the user-centred principles of hypertext design outlined, the present chapter describes some of the work we have carried out in building a hypertext database.

This database is intended to support research workers' uses of specialist literature. The ultimate aim of this work is to investigate the primary real world issue — is a hypertext database of significant use to the people who would normally use the paper-based version of the information? However, the project itself offers a valid method of testing the merits of our own approach, i.e., user-centred design, and shedding light on many of the issues described in the preceding chapters.

In the environment in which many scientific researchers work, the various professional journals form the largest single paper-based resource, so this was selected as a realistic information space for investigation. In order to evaluate the possibilities of a journal in hypertext format, it was decided to create an electronic version of the journal *Behaviour and Information Technology* (BIT). This journal publishes papers concerning the human factors issues associated with the introduction of information technology, and its readership is typically composed of psychologists, ergonomists and computer scientists. The academic sub-discipline of human-computer factors is relatively recent and the majority of relevant papers are published in only a handful of journals. Thus, by creating an electronic version of just one of these journals, an appreciable proportion of the literature could be made available for experimental investigation using actual readers and realistic tasks. Furthermore, as this was our own specialist domain we were in a position to test its suitability with colleagues who would be less susceptible to the Hawthorne effect or the pressures of politeness in providing us with feedback!

Following the granting of limited copyright permission from the publishers, all the back issues of BIT were scanned and the resulting computer files subjected to optical character recognition processing. In this way the full text and graphics for all the articles were made available for presentation as a hypertext database.

As outlined earlier in the book, the first step in developing any hypertext system is to identify and understand as much as possible the *users*, their *tasks* and the *information* space. In the following sections we examine this preliminary work aimed at developing a suitable specification of the database. The issues considered, analytic techniques employed and implications drawn for the development of the system are also outlined.

System specification: understanding the users, tasks and information space

The Users

The intended user population was human factors researchers so we started with those working at our research institute in Loughborough. These are professionals with relevant degrees who are experienced users of both information technology and the text type considered here. As such we expected few difficulties in encouraging use of a suitable application, and we were fairly sure that such a database could satisfy a proven information need. However, it should be noted that these users are not dedicated technologists but people who will learn to use a system if and only if it satisfies a need.

The Task

While it might seem at first glance that journal articles are used in a relatively predictable fashion, there is little evidence to support such a view; as we outlined in Chapter 3, such assumptions on usage styles are rarely justified. Thus, to gain insight into the task issues, a study of journal usage was carried out on a sample of regular journal readers interacting with a variety of articles (full details of this study are published in Dillon *et al.*, 1989). In general, the results indicated that readers develop strategies for scanning an issue of a journal in order to look for salient articles, e.g., searching the list of authors for familiar names or lists of titles for relevant topics. Furthermore, the journal articles themselves are subjected to relatively consistent forms of use by readers. When an article of interest is identified, then the reader opens the journal at the start of the relevant paper and adopts one of three reading strategies.

In the first case, the abstract is usually attended to and a decision made about the suitability of the article for the reader's purposes. At this point, most readers reported also browsing the start of the introduction before flicking through the article to get a better impression of the contents. Readers reported attending to the section headings, the diagrams and tables, noting both the level of mathematical content and the length of the article. Browsing the conclusions also seems to be a common method of extracting central ideas from the article and deciding on its worth.

The second strategy involved reading the article in a non-serial fashion to rapidly extract relevant information. This involved reading some sections fully and only skimming or even skipping others. Typically, the method and results sections of experimental papers are skim-read, while the introduction or introductory sections and the discussion/conclusions are read fully.

The final strategy is a serial, detailed read from start to finish. This was seen as "studying" the article's contents and, though not carried out for each article that is selected, most subjects reported that they usually read selected articles at this level of detail eventually.

While individual preferences for a strategy were reported, most readers seem to use both the second and third strategies depending on the task or purpose for reading the article, time available and the content of the article. Original and interesting work is more likely to be read fully than dull or routine papers. Reading to keep up with the literature requires less "studying" of articles than that required in attempting to understand a new area. However, even when reading at the third level, some subjects still reported skimming particular sections that were not intrinsically relevant to their particular needs at that time.

Thus, readers perform a variety of tasks with journal articles, from scanning for specific information to studying the contents in depth, and these tasks require interactions with the text lasting from a few seconds to an hour or more. Manipulations of the paper may be simple (e.g., turning a page) or complex (jumping to a particular section while keeping a marker in another).

The information space

In Chapter 4 we discussed the notion of readers' models of text structure and schemas of typical document forms. In particular, we described two studies by Dillon (1989) looking at subjects piecing together journal articles which had been physically cut up or naming the likely location of isolated sentences of text presented on paper and screen. These studies were carried out as part of this database development process but will not be described further here.

These findings have direct relevance to the development of hypertext articles in that they suggest that drastically altering the structure of the text would not aid the reader. Rather, the reader's model should be supported by the hypertext version as a way of aiding usage. Experienced readers of journal articles have a well-developed superstructure or schema of the text's likely form which they use for purposes of navigation and information location. In conjunction with the findings from the study on how articles are used, these results suggest that hypertext articles have the potential to support several of the tasks which readers perform and greatly enhance the rate of access to stored material.

It should be noted at this point that this set of studies was carried out on a sample of the target end-user population, i.e., people who were likely to be using the system once it had been built. This ensured that any findings were directly relevant to the users of the technology. Understanding and designing a usable hypertext application requires knowledge of the users, their tasks and the information space under consideration. These studies have provided relevant information on all three of these aspects. We know who the users are, what type of tasks they perform with the text and how they perform them. We have also identified the target readers' schemas of the information space and can use this information to inform the design of the hypertext articles' structure. The following section describes the first implementation.

The structure of the database

Electronic journals are likely to offer some improvements for particular task scenarios but none in others. For example, electronic storage and retrieval should make access to material easier and faster, thus offering a distinct advantage over paper. However, at the article level, given what we know about reading from screens, merely reproducing the linear format of the text on screen is unlikely to encourage use, and paper will certainly be preferred for tasks requiring serial reading of lengthy sections.[1] Structuring the presentation on screen in ways not available on paper may be the answer, which brings us to the consideration of readers' models or schemas for the information space.

The database is composed of two distinct hypertext modules: a 'front-end'

---

[1]   A study by Dillon (1990b) showed that when sections of text larger than a screenful were being scanned for particular information, paper was significantly faster than hypertext.

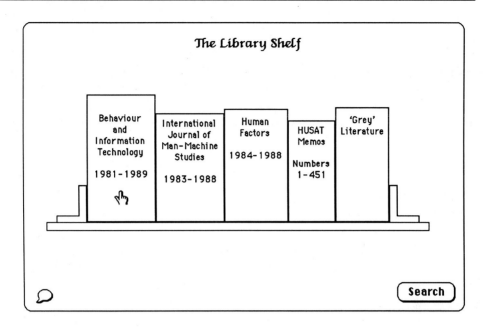

Figure 14: The library shelf from which journals can be selected.

structured in HyperCard and the body of journal articles which are formatted as individual Guide documents. The database architecture reflects the distinct components of reading identified in the journal usage study: an initial period of searching or browsing at the title and author level which typically results in a decision to read a piece of text (perhaps only briefly) and also allows for the serendipitous discovery of articles. The text is then sampled repeatedly until a higher order decision can be made with a degree of confidence concerning its suitability for a particular information requirement ("this text does/does not contain the information that I want"). At this stage, a more continuous style of reading is likely to be adopted for particular sections of the text, or the article will be abandoned and the reader will return to the top level, possibly to repeat the process.

The database front-end
The initial view of the database consists of a graphical representation of a library shelf with the spines of various selectable journals and associated literature visible (see Figure 14). Such a representation has the advantage that it draws on a wealth of experience which users already have — all target users understand a library shelf at a local level. However, the categorisation of books often seems arbitrary to

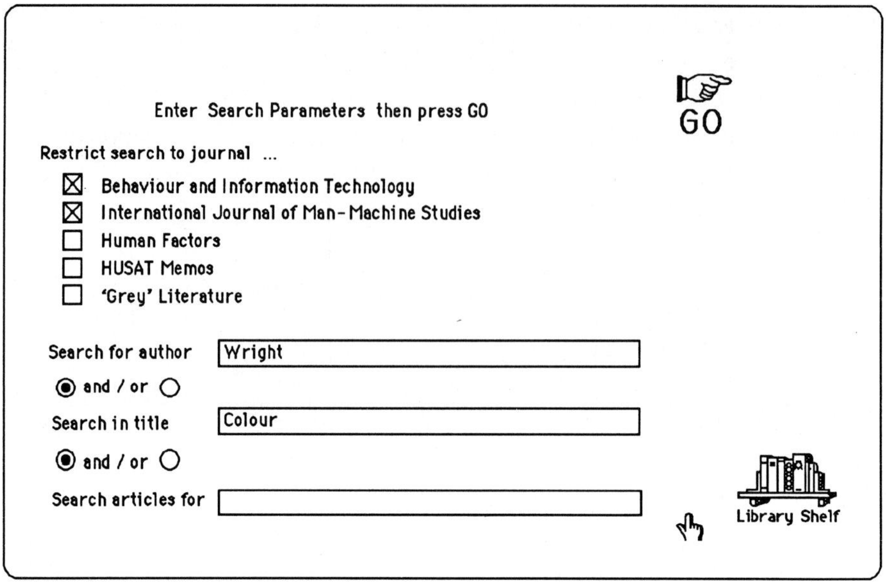

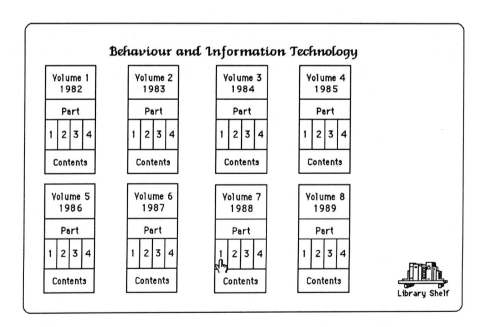

Figure 15: The search facilities operate across the entire database.

Figure 16: The available volumes of the selected journal.

non-librarians and can result in semantically related books being distributed across widely separated shelves. Thus, this simple visual metaphor is not necessarily the optimum form of representation and would not be appropriate for a much larger database. For this reason, alternatives such as concept maps or semantic nets should be experimentally evaluated. Access to a search option is offered at the top level, which allows a string search of the author and title fields and the full text of the journal articles (see Figure 15).

Selecting a journal from the shelf leads to the display of a schematic browser for the complete contents of the journal in terms of the various volumes and parts (see Figure 16). Two means of accessing the individual articles are offered at this stage: a series of volume indices which alphabetically list the authors and titles, selected by clicking in the "contents" area of the display; or issue/part contents lists which present the author and title details in the same order as the paper original (see Figure 17), obtained by clicking in the relevant numbered section. Selecting an article from either display results in the launch of the Guide software and the presentation of the top level of the chosen article.

The structure of the articles
The individual articles are organized hierarchically and the top level consists of the title page details plus the major headings of the article (see Figure 18). With the exception of the title all these items are selectable. Choosing an item with the mouse causes the text 'folded' underneath to be displayed at that point and the length of the document increases proportionally. The text that is unfolded may itself contain further 'buttons' (subheadings, figures and tables) and this process can therefore be repeated until the full text of the article has been unfolded and is displayed on screen as a linear, scrollable document.

A second type of embedding is used to display the equivalent of electronic footnotes. Selecting many of the references in the text causes a window to appear temporarily on the screen with the full bibliographic details of the reference displayed (see Figure 19). This facility was included in order to support the often-observed technique which readers employ — that of keeping a finger in the references section and turning to it briefly when a reference is encountered in the text.

If a reference is made to another article in the database, then selecting it results in a separate window being opened and the display of the article as a new Guide document. If the reader quits from Guide then all the documents are closed and the reader is returned to the top level HyperCard browser at the point from which they launched the first document.

By maintaining the same structural components of the articles (abstract,

Behaviour and Information Technology 1988 : Volume 7 Part 1
Legibility of video display units during off-angle viewing.
S.J. Morrissey & R.W. Chu
Colour cues as location aids in lengthy texts on screen and paper.
P. Wright & A. Lickorish
Selected graph design variables in four interpretation tasks: a microcomputer-based pilot study.
J.G. Casali & K.B. Gaylin
The effect of tree structure on search in a hierarchical menu selection system.
K.L. Norman & J.P. Chin
Monitoring computer users' behaviour in office environments.
A.L. Teubner & J.J. Yaske
Users' experiences of COM — a computer-mediated communication system.
L. Adrianson & E. Hjelmquist

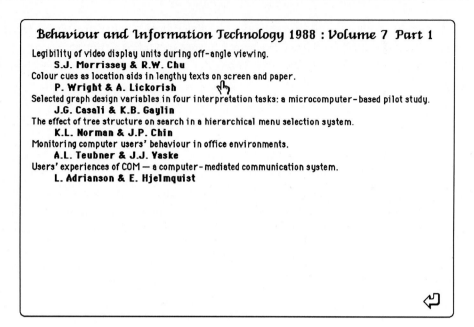

Figure 17: The contents of a selected issue in the same order as the paper original.

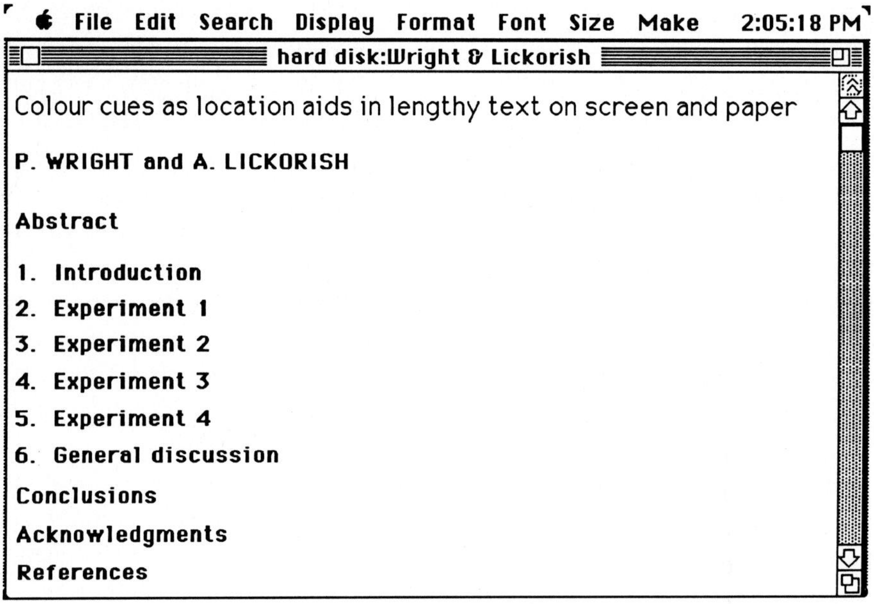

File Edit Search Display Format Font Size Make 2:05:18 PM
hard disk:Wright & Lickorish
Colour cues as location aids in lengthy text on screen and paper
P. WRIGHT and A. LICKORISH
Abstract
1. Introduction
2. Experiment 1
3. Experiment 2
4. Experiment 3
5. Experiment 4
6. General discussion
Conclusions
Acknowledgments
References

Figure 18: The top level of the selected article. Each heading is a 'button'.

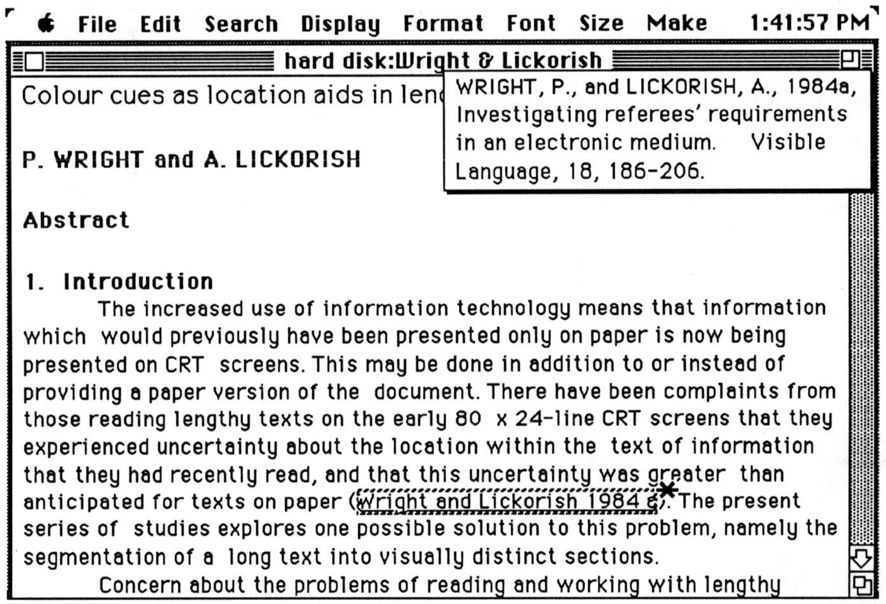

```
 ⌐ ⌂  File  Edit  Search  Display  Format  Font  Size  Make    1:41:57 PM⌐
┌──────────────────────── hard disk:Wright & Lickorish ────────────────────┐
│ Colour cues as location aids in len┌─────────────────────────────────┐   │
│                                     │WRIGHT, P., and LICKORISH, A., 1984a,│ │
│                                     │Investigating referees' requirements│ │
│ P. WRIGHT and A. LICKORISH          │in an electronic medium.    Visible│ │
│                                     │Language, 18, 186-206.            │   │
│                                     └─────────────────────────────────┘   │
│ Abstract                                                                  │
│                                                                           │
│ 1. Introduction                                                           │
│       The increased use of information technology means that information  │
│ which  would previously have been presented only on paper is now being    │
│ presented on CRT  screens. This may be done in addition to or instead of  │
│ providing a paper version of the  document. There have been complaints from│
│ those reading lengthy texts on the early 80 x 24-line CRT screens that they│
│ experienced uncertainty about the location within the  text of information │
│ that they had recently read, and that this uncertainty was greater  than  │
│ anticipated for texts on paper (Wright and Lickorish 1984 a). The present │
│ series of  studies explores one possible solution to this problem, namely the│
│ segmentation of a  long text into visually distinct sections.             │
│       Concern about the problems of reading and working with lengthy      │
└───────────────────────────────────────────────────────────────────────────┘
```

Figure 19: Bibliographic details appear in a pop-up window (top right).

introduction, discussion and so forth), the database does not force the user to abandon an existing schema and develop a new one. Users know what to expect in a results section and the database design does not surprise them. What it *does* offer is a way of accessing the relevant information rapidly.

The interface for accessing the documents and the structure of the individual articles are designed to support and enhance the reading strategies identified in the paper journal usage study. Readers can rapidly scan the contents lists in the same way as they do with paper journals but they also have the ability to search the complete set of authors and titles to find, for example, a specific article when only a few details of the title or authors are known; or the search can be limited to all the papers by a given author or all the papers with a specific keyword in the title, or even any article which includes a given term in the actual text. While searching for particular authors is simple but laborious using the paper version, searching for all articles which contain a particular term is totally impractical without an electronic version.

Similarly, the hierarchical structure of the journal articles is designed to support the reader while 'manipulating' the document. It is not true that "readers access most text in serial order" (Jonassen, 1986) except at the obvious sentence level. The journal usage study indicated that readers very rarely read articles serially, preferring to 'jump about' from section to section, typically from the introduction to the references or discussion.

The hierarchical format supported by Guide allows readers to access directly the sections of the document that are of particular interest without the possible distraction of having to search through the entire text. Thus, a reader can select and the skim-read the abstract, conclusion or even only the references. If more detailed reading is warranted then not only is the full text available but it is also possible to follow up references to other papers immediately to check on the author's interpretation of the results or even the experimental details themselves. In other words, when a reference to another article that appears in the database is cited in one article, the user can action a direct link to the full text of the cited article if they so wish. This has obvious advantages in situations where the user is trying to trace the development of a concept or argument through several independent texts.

Testing the design

The design of the database has been the subject of some pilot evaluations on samples of the target users. Typically these have involved a small sample of the target user population familiarising themselves with the database and/or performing representative tasks. Such trials were deemed more relevant than formal experimental trials at this stage of the design process. In the first instance, the evaluations have been primarily concerned with whether or not people can use the database sensibly (i.e., can they use it for a task they wish to perform). These have indicated that the design is viewed favourably by the target users, and is seen as easy to learn and use for individuals with some experience of Macintosh-style WIMP[2] interfaces. This initial success is attributable to the manner in which the system embodies the user's natural style of interaction with this type of text as detailed in the task analysis.

The ability to access instantly the total contents of a journal from one's desk is seen as a major advantage. However, as we have noted elsewhere (Richardson *et al.*, 1988), individuals have difficulties with search facilities and this limits their use of such a system. Jumping to other articles is an issue that requires investigation because it is not always the case that readers want the full contents of another article; an abstract or relevant section of the selected text may be sufficient. Obviously, we need research on the sort of searches that users wish to perform with this material. Also, the current implementation of the database is weak in

---

2   WIMP is an acronym for Windows, Icons, Menus and Pointing device, or alternatively, Windows, Icons, Mouse and Pull-down menus. It refers to the style of interface typically found in many systems which simulate desktops.

terms of the navigation information required to support jumping between articles. This is the first area for re-design.

At this stage we know that we are on the right lines. Minor modifications and evaluations of the search facilities would be a logical next step. Obviously further evaluations must be carried out before we can be confident that this system is viable. The next major test is to offer the database as a resource in the HUSAT library for use by human factors researchers to see how it is used in real task situations. Ultimately we envisage readers accessing it on their desktop via the computer network but only after we have demonstrated its usability and utility to intended users. The design process enters another iteration!

Conclusion

While the database is interesting, the main aim of this chapter was to highlight the manner in which the issues discussed in this book might be applied in the domain of application design. Issues pertaining to characteristic task performance, navigation, readers' models of the information space, text type and so forth are not mere theoretical concepts, interesting to speculate upon but ultimately difficult to utilise in the real-world of database building. This chapter not only describes our conviction in them but also our application of them through standard or modified task analysis and experimental techniques. The responses to the subsequent design have been favourable, a fact we attribute to the design methods employed.

We are certain that systems like this will have an increasingly important rôle to play in scholarly information exchange in the future. As in all technological developments, there will be many instances of poor design emerging — systems that might be capable of performing previously difficult or impossible tasks but in failing to consider the users, their tasks and information spaces properly fall short of delivering any real benefits to users. However, well designed systems offer the potential for significant improvements in some aspects of information usage. The approach adopted here, which might loosely be termed user-centred design, is the best way of avoiding the pitfalls.

For those readers unlikely ever to be involved in designing systems themselves, the approach is useful for considering how acceptable they find any technology. A system is not good because it is expensive, or because you are told it is, or because it is hypertext! It is good only to the extent that it suits your needs. If you cannot use it, blame the designer, not yourself.

CHAPTER EIGHT

WHERE DO WE GO FROM HERE?

"This is not the end. It is not even the beginning of the end. But it is, perhaps, the end of the beginning."

Winston Churchill

Our aim in this chapter is *not* to predict the future of hypertext. The history of technological development is littered with predictions which, at the time and from a particular perspective, might have seemed reasonable but which, with the advantage of hindsight, have proved to be nonsense. The prediction that railway trains could go no faster than 12 miles per hour without the passengers being sucked out of the windows is a good example, and we have no desire to make such predictions in a field which relies on computer science, where the speed of change is often faster than the speed of the publishing process — "by the time you read this, it's out of date!"

Rather, we will attempt to highlight some of the areas in which development would seem to be desirable and also discuss some of the 'new' extensions to hypertext which are currently being researched. Finally, we will offer our 'position statement' on hypertext.

New extensions

Computer Supported Collaborative Work
The field of Computer Supported Collaborative Work (CSCW) extends far beyond hypertext and is the subject of its own international conferences. However, it is of interest here because several people have ventured to suggest that hypertext

technology might support CSCW in unique ways. For example, Brown (1988) points to collaborative authorship as one of nine areas which provide "opportunities for challenging research projects" and Halasz (1987) lists support for collaborative work as one of seven issues for "the next generation of hypermedia systems."

As we mentioned in Chapter 1, Randall Trigg has been involved in using NoteCards for collaborative authoring and in particular he and Lucy Suchman have reported their own experiences in collaborating within a NoteCard environment (Trigg and Suchman, 1989). They found it necessary to 'invent' different kinds of cards in addition to those which existed in the single-user environment. For example, History cards were devised in order to keep track of changes which either had made to the documents they were working on; Message cards were invented to support a higher-level discussion about the *procedures* of collaboration (as opposed to the *content* of the collaboration).

We are currently involved in a project funded by the British Library Research and Development Department which, in its second phase, aims to study the appropriateness of hypertext for supporting the work of a research team. We can foresee several issues which will require clarification and resolution if the medium is to be used successfully. For example, in a research team involving several members, is it necessary to differentiate between the inputs of the different members? If so, how can this be achieved? With a small number of authors it would be possible to allocate a different font to each author, but as the number of authors increases this 'solution' becomes increasingly infeasible. Similarly, colour could be used to identify each author's input but only if a small number of authors are involved.

A related problem to the identification of authors is that of the 'weight' attached to each author's input. For example, does the input of the professor in charge of the research team carry the same weight as that of the junior research assistant? Similarly, who has 'editing rights'? In a discussion document it is desirable that alternative views are presented, but if the document is a report to a client then it may be more important to present a unified front.

Clearly, then, CSCW is an area in which hypertext has a potential contribution to make but in which there are issues yet to be resolved. It is possible that it is only feasible for certain types of group working or for the production of certain kinds of documents. It may even be the case that hypertext supports the brainstorming and initial idea-generating phases of document production, where the precise structure is not important, but doesn't support the later phase where structure becomes paramount. We would not be surprised to discover such task specificity in the light of the views we have represented in earlier chapters.

Intelligent hypertext

Rada and Barlow (1989) suggest the term 'expertext' to refer to systems which combine expert systems and hypertext. Such a combination is intended to embody the semantic richness of hypertext with the specifiable, computable links of expert systems. The aim of the expert system aspect is to provide 'guidance' for the user, an aim which at first sight might seem antithetical to the 'free range' spirit of hypertext. However, Diaper and Rada (1989) argue that the combination offers the possibility of sensibly distributing the labour between the human and machine intelligence. Unfortunately there is little empirical evidence for the utility of expert systems, based as they are on an extremely restricted understanding of human knowledge utilisation and decision making. However, expertext represents the absorbing of hypertext ideas into other fields, the use of what we might term a hypertext interface, and this is a trend which we feel will continue.

Kibby and Mayes (1989) also describe their StrathTutor system as approaching intelligent hypertext. The 'intelligence' is seen to reside in the fact that links are not fixed in StrathTutor but rather are computed on the basis of where the reader is and where they have been before. However, as Kibby and Mayes admit, such ideas can be implemented in small hypertexts but become increasingly difficult as the size of the hypertext increases. Furthermore, the calculations which determine the links are based on the description of each frame on a number of attributes. While authors can easily make (and un-make) fixed links in most systems, few would wish to rate each frame on any number of attributes (leaving aside the question of how we derive the appropriate list of attributes in the first place).

Nevertheless, StrathTutor does offer some advantages over the fixed link approach. For example, deleting a frame does not necessitate making sure that all links to that frame are also deleted. Similarly, adding a frame (and its ratings on the attribute set) is simple and it will automatically be included in the calculations next time the system is run. Whether the system should be labelled 'intelligent' is open to debate.

Developments needed

Experience

At the most basic level, there is a need for both authors and readers to gain experience of hypertext. Readers of paper documents have a wealth of experience of document types (from comics to textbooks), have developed a variety of reading strategies and manipulation techniques. It will require use of hypertext over some time before users begin to develop the equivalent skills in hypertext. Most people's experience of electronic documents will have been via word processors, and while this may lead to a general familiarity with microcomputers it is not an appropriate model for hypertext and hence negative transfer[1] may occur. Such negative transfer will work against the acceptance of hypertext and demands that the maximum support be given to the beginning user via the interface, navigation mechanisms and manipulation techniques. The well-documented preference for reading from paper rather than screen may well decline as screen technology improves, but only if the reading interfaces support the reader's tasks.

Similarly, authors have developed skills which may not be totally appropriate to hypertext and will have to learn a new set of skills. Even with the prevalence of word processors, many people still say that they prefer to write on paper in the first instance, transferring the text to the machine at a later stage, and the same may be true of hypertext. It is also not clear that the electronic medium in general or hypertext in particular can support the range of idiosyncrasies observed in many creative authors.[2] The paper medium has been tolerant of such behaviour because it was not evident in the finished product. However, since hypertext depends so heavily on the computer, authors will presumably need to develop their skills in direct interaction with the computer.

Software Tools

Both reader and author require appropriate tools for use in the hypertext environment, and to a large extent such tools have not yet been developed. For the reader, such tools need to support operations such as manipulation, linking and annotation in order that the hypertext can be used effectively, personalised in the same way that photocopies are at present. It would probably help the reader of hypertext if a common user interface were employed across applications, but this is unlikely to occur for a number of reasons. Firstly, hypertext packages are increasingly software products, sold by companies who have invested time and money in their development. It is important to manufacturers that their own products are distinctive and that they do *not* look too similar to their competitors' products, as evidenced by the 'look and feel' lawsuits filed by various software companies against each other. It is likely, therefore, that the level of commonality

---

1   Negative transfer is the effect whereby learning one task has a detrimental effect on the subsequent learning of some other task.

2   Ernest Hemingway wrote while standing up, and preferred to be standing on the skin of a lesser kudu while he wrote. Flaubert would go into the hall of his house and shout what he had written, arguing that if it sounded good in the form of a bellow it would succeed on the page. Even modern authors have their foibles. Truman Capote can't work in a room containing yellow roses or if there are three cigarette butts in the ashtray. Muriel Spark writes on pale blue jotters that she can only buy from a stationers in the Royal Mile in Edinburgh.

between applications is no more than that which already exists on machines such as the Apple Macintosh, i.e., the general WIMP interface. The example of existing word processing packages on the Macintosh serves to reinforce this view. Although they all have a common core of functionality, they differ greatly in terms of the way they look on screen and the way in which the various operations are performed (compare, for example, FullWrite Professional and Microsoft Word 4). At this level, Guide and HyperCard have a common user interface (if we ignore the fact that HyperCard violates several of Apple's own interface guidelines). However, to the user they are as alike as chalk and cheese. Of course, the desirability of a completely common user interface may be questioned on the grounds that we have raised earlier, that the different packages have different strengths and weaknesses and we should expect each to support some tasks better than others (and none to support all tasks).

From the author's point of view, a variety of software tools to support hypertext authoring would be desirable. For example, in various systems we have seen authors generate such 'violations' as the self-referential link which points back to the same frame as it originates from; the dangling link which points into what might best be described as hyperspace (and the variant, mentioned by Brown (1988) which points to a reminder to 'fill this in later'); and isolated nodes which are not linked to any others and are therefore inaccessible in the normal course of events. Such problems also exist to some extent in the paper medium, for example referring to an author in the text of an article and then omitting to include the appropriate reference, or conversely including a reference to an author who is not mentioned in the text. However, in the paper medium it is relatively easy to check such things during a proof-reading stage. In a complex hypertext, it would be desirable to delegate such consistency checks to the system. It is probably because the majority of hypertexts in existence are the result of transferring existing information from paper to hypertext that authoring problems have not achieved greater prominence. As an increasing number of documents are originated in hypertext we would expect an increasing number of problems to be revealed.

Hypertext in Context: what have we learned?

Hopefully, the preceding chapters have helped to place the phenomenon of hypertext in the wider context of information storage and retrieval systems which are themselves used in a variety of situations. We will now therefore attempt to summarise our position regarding hypertext. Like any position statement, it is open to argument and discussion. It has been arrived at as a result of some three or four years thinking about the issues, conducting experiments, attending conferences, reading and listening to others' views, designing and building hypertexts. Since we will continue to carry out such activities, it is only to be expected that our position may change as a result of experience — if it did not it would be a dogma rather than a position. Hence, what follows is 'where we are now'.

The ideas behind hypertext are far from new, and even some of the computer-based instantiations are 25 years old. However, hypertext has become *popular* since the availability of powerful desktop micros has increased. Unfortunately, more has been claimed for hypertext than the facts support. One particular claim, linked to the 'paperless office' notion, is that hypertext 'frees us from the paper chains of linear text'. In our view, throughout the recent literature of hypertext, paper has had a bad press! Printed texts are generally *not* linear, either in their semantic structure or in the way in which skilled readers use them. Hence, to claim that hypertext frees us from the confines of paper is to tilt at windmills. Electronic documentation, whether structured using hypertext techniques or not, will not replace paper in the short-to-medium term. If paper is replaced in the long term it will be as much for socio-economic reasons (depletion of resources necessary for its manufacture, falling price of alternatives) as for conceptual reasons.

Hypertext is not a universal panacea, nor is it so rigidly defined as to allow only a single style of implementation. Hence, some implementations will support some tasks, but none will support all tasks. It is the nature of the interaction between user, task and tool that will determine performance. In the same way that different text types have evolved in the paper medium, we would expect different types to evolve in the electronic medium. The question is the extent to which hypertext has a rôle to play in this evolutionary process.

Although possibly over-emphasised by some authors, navigation *is* a potential problem in using hypertext and cannot be ignored. However, it is not a problem unique to hypertext and many people make a decent living acting as guides in the maze of paper documentation.

Since many hypertexts will be created by the transferring of existing information, methods need to be developed to automate this process. Without such methods, the hypertexts available for research purposes will continue to be small and therefore only allow a restricted range of research questions to be addressed.

Hypertext is, above all, an access mechanism and as such has a potential rôle to play in all situations where information is accessed and used, including the educational environment. It is 'a way of thinking about' structuring information and as such will probably cease to be called hypertext in the near future, as the ideas get absorbed into many informational contexts and designed into the interfaces to a variety of computer-based working environments. The success of the ideas will be judged on their ability to help people achieve their aims.

GLOSSARY

Document Examiner

The Document Examiner is part of the Genera operating system which runs on Symbolics computers. The system is used to deliver the operating system's technical documentation which runs to some 8,000 printed pages, and this means that it is one of the first major hypertext systems. While the system contains many standard hypertext features — a windowing system with a node-and-link data structure — information is presented to the user in 'pages' which include many of the typographic characteristics of printed books.

Walker, J.H. (1987) Document Examiner: delivery interface for hypertext documents. *Proceedings of Hypertext '87*. University of North Carolina, Chapel Hill. 307–323.

gIBIS

gIBIS stands for Graphical Issue Based Information System and refers to a hypertext system developed at the Microelectronics and Computer Technology Corporation (MCC) with a specific application in mind, namely the representation of initial design ideas. The system is designed for network use and falls squarely within the range of applications which underlie the emerging area of computer supported collaborative work. The gIBIS system is capable of capturing, storing and retrieving informal graphical designs in support of the design process.

Conklin, J. and Begeman, M.L. (1989) gIBIS: a tool for all reasons. *Journal of the American Society for Information Science*, 40(3), 200–213.

Glasgow On-Line

Glasgow On-Line is a major hypertext project that has used Apple's HyperCard system to construct a comprehensive guide to the City of Glasgow for residents as well as visitors. The database is designed for public access, and ease of use has been a primary interest.

Baird, P. and Percival, M. (1989) Glasgow On-Line: database development using Apple's HyperCard. In R. McAleese (ed.) *Hypertext: Theory into Practice*. Oxford: Intellect.

Guide

Guide was developed by Peter Brown at the University of Kent in the early 1980s and was subsequently marketed by Office Workstations Limited (OWL) as one of the first hypertext systems for both IBM PC and Apple Macintosh computers. The system has a strong hierarchical data model which can best be described as an extendable scroll. Units of text or graphics of variable size can be 'folded' beneath buttons in the hypertext and the selection of these buttons with the mouse pointing device causes the hidden text to be displayed at that point. This has the effect of lengthening the displayed hypertext, which can then be viewed by scrolling. The system is frequently recommended for use with hierarchically structured documents which can be collapsed so that the reader is initially presented with only the top level contents items. The reader can then proceed down through the hierarchy of headings and subheadings and thus sees only the portion of the text which is of specific interest. Other features include on screen notes in pop-up windows and reference links to other sections of the same or distinct documents.

Brown, P.J. (1987) Turning ideas into products: the Guide system. In *Proceedings of Hypertext '87*. University of North Carolina, Chapel Hill. 33–40.

HyperCard

Apple's HyperCard was first released in 1987 and is currently supplied with all new Macintosh computers. HyperCard is frequently misunderstood to be a hypertext system but it is in fact an application generator which can be used, among many other things, to construct hypertexts. HyperCard is very flexible, but some features are common to all the applications (or 'stacks'). The data model consist of a series of standard sized cards which comprise a consistent background but differing foregrounds of text or bit-mapped graphic. Buttons displayed on the foreground allow linked cards to be displayed sequentially according to a 'script' with a variety of effects — some of which approach animation.

Goodman, D. (1987) *The Complete HyperCard Handbook*. New York: Bantam Books.

Hyperlog

Hyperlog is probably the first hypertext system to emerge from the USSR. It is implemented in Revelation Database Application Environment and runs on an IBM PC/XT or AT under DOS. The system consists of standard nodes and links but the rhetoric of interaction is based on 'issues' which users can specify, choose or create, which are then 'unfolded' according to the path taken. The application also supports writing and link formation.

No published references are currently available, but interested parties should contact Professor Lakayev, GKVTI, Presnensky Val 19, Moscow 123557.

HyperTIES

HyperTIES originated in 1983 as a research project at the University of Maryland under the direction of Ben Shneiderman and was originally called TIES (The Interactive Encyclopedia System). The commercial version runs on IBM PC computers under the standard DOS operating system and has a very simple cursor-key controlled user interface. It is expressly designed with ease of use in mind and has had a number of applications developed for use in public places. A HyperTIES database consists of an encyclopædia of up to 200 interlinked files. Only one type of link is supported and this connects a highlighted word in one 'article' (i.e., file) to another article. Since the destination node is the article rather than a sub-element, there is an obvious pressure to minimise article length so that link relevance is maintained. The system automatically generates an alphabetical index of articles which can be browsed by the reader.

Shneiderman, B. (1987) User interface design and evaluation for an electronic encyclopedia. In G. Salvendy (ed.) *Cognitive Engineering in the Design of Human-Computer Interaction and Expert Systems.* Amsterdam: Elsevier.

Intermedia

Intermedia is the latest in a series of hypertext like systems to emerge from the Institute for Research in Information and Scholarship (IRIS) at Brown University. Intermedia is a multimedia teaching environment and is an umbrella term for a variety of text and graphics based applications. Used in combination, they allow teachers to construct electronic courses which can be explored, and commented upon, by their students. Intermedia incorporates the concept of *webs* which are sub-assemblies of the total hypertext network. When a given web is invoked, only the links between nodes which are relevant to that web are displayed. This allows different teachers to construct a variety of arguments using the same basic material.

Yankelovich, N., Haan, B.J., Meyrowitz, N. and Drucker, S.M. (1985) Intermedia: the concept and the construction of a seamless information environment. *Computer*, January, 81–96.

KMS

A commercial implementation marketed by Knowledge Systems resulting from the ZOG system developed at Carnegie Mellon University between 1972 – 1985. The system runs on networks of advanced Sun and Apollo workstations and has been used for a variety of collaborative applications, e.g., on-line documentation, publishing, and software engineering. The user interface is highly consistent across different applications and comprises a set of 'frames' linked in a hierarchical network. The complete command set for database navigation and editing can be invoked via a three-button mouse. The designers claim that the consistent interface, the pronounced hierarchical structure and fast system response time all help prevent the user from getting lost.

Akscyn, R.M., McCracken, D.N. and Yoder, E.A. (1988) KMS: a distributed hypermedia system for managing knowledge in organizations. *Communications of the ACM*, 31(7), 820–835.

NLS/Augment

NLS (or oN Line System) is a seminal and highly ambitious research support tool created in 1968 by Doug Engelbart at the Augmented Human Intellect Research Centre, part of the Stanford Research Institute. The system was intended to be a complete computer environment for supporting all the aspects of the researcher's activities (i.e., text storage, manipulation and access, software design and debugging, and intercommunication.) and 'augmenting' his intellect. NLS was intended as a specialist's tool with a commitment from the user to master unique input devices, and was responsible for introducing the mouse to the computing community. The system is now sold by McDonnell-Douglas and the major user is the US Air Force.

Engelbart, D.C. and English, W.K. (1968) A research center for augmenting human intellect. *Proceedings of the AFIPS Fall Joint Computer Conference*. Montvale, NJ: AFIPS Press.

NoteCards

NoteCards was developed as a research tool at the Xerox Palo Alto Research Centre by Frank Halasz, Randy Trigg and Tom Moran. The system is based on the familiar concept of the card file index which is represented electronically as a set of *NoteCards* of variable size. Each notecard can contain text or graphics and can be linked to other notecards via 'typed' links. Notecards can be organized by way of *Fileboxes* (groups of cards) and *Browsers* (structural maps of linked notecards). NoteCards has proved an effective tool for organizing and analysing information since it is easy to construct and revise a variety of possible structures for a collection of low level items. The system runs on Xerox Workstations under LISP and has been highly influential but has not achieved widespread usage except within the Xerox corporation.

Halasz, F.G., Moran, T.P. and Trigg, R.H. (1987) NoteCards in a nutshell. *Proceedings of the ACM CHI+GI Conference*, Toronto. 45–52.

StrathTutor

Developed at the University of Strathclyde, StrathTutor is based on Hintzman's model of human memory. It is a frame-based 'learning-by-browsing' system, but differs from other hypertext systems in that there are no explicit links between frames. At the time of authoring, each frame is rated on up to 60 attributes and links are then calculated at run-time using pattern matching heuristics, according to the type of interaction which the learner initiates. A major advantage of the lack of fixed links is that editing of the frame-base is relatively easy — deleted frames do not leave 'dangling' links and added frames are automatically incorporated at the next run-time.

Kibby, M.R. and Mayes, J.T. (1989) Towards intelligent hypertext. In R. McAleese (ed.) *Hypertext: Theory into Practice*. Oxford: Intellect.

SuperBook

SuperBook, developed at the Bell Communications Research laboratory (BellCoRe), is a browsing system for electronic texts prepared for paper publication using proprietary systems such as Interleaf, Scribe or troff. SuperBook's aim is to enhance the retrieval of information from existing electronic texts without the added demand of converting them into a specific hypertext format. When the text is viewed using SuperBook, a multi-window display is created which shows the text, a fully selectable contents 'page' and a window for conducting sophisticated string searching. The developers concede that SuperBook may fall beyond some people's definition of hypertext since it makes no pretensions to being a system for text authoring.

Remde, J.R., Gomez, L.M. and Landauer, T.K. (1987) SuperBook: an automatic tool for information exploration — hypertext? In *Proceedings of Hypertext '87*. University of North Carolina, Chapel Hill. 175–188.

Thoth-II

Thoth-II, like Document Examiner, runs on Symbolics' Lisp machines and makes full use of the sophisticated facilities that the interface offers. A key feature of this system is the concept of the labelled directed graph. While the concept is a general one and by no means unique to Thoth-II, it is a design goal of the system that semantic relationships between entities should be explicit. Thoth-II thus represents an attempt to reduce the requirement/opportunity for the reader to interpret the structure of the hypertext.

Collier, G.H. (1987) Thoth-II: hypertext with explicit semantics. In *Proceedings of Hypertext '87*. University of North Carolina, Chapel Hill. 269–289.

Writing Environment (WE)

This system has been developed at the University of North Carolina with the specific aim of supporting the writing process. The system's design has been influenced by a psychological analysis of the comprehension process which assumes that the linear sequences of words and sentences are assembled into semantic hierarchies by the reader and subsequently stored in long term memory as networks. WE is designed to support the writer perform the reverse of this comprehension process, i.e., imposing a hierarchical discipline on networks of loosely structured concepts and then building an essentially linear sequence of sentences. WE includes a variety of ways of viewing and structuring text nodes and can be seen to be closely related to NoteCards in this respect.

Smith, J.B., Weiss, S.F. and Ferguson, G.J. (1987) A hypertext writing environment and its cognitive basis. In *Proceedings of Hypertext '87*. University of North Carolina, Chapel Hill. 195–214.

Xanadu

The Xanadu system is the long term hypertext project inspired and pursued by Ted Nelson. His aim is simply to design a network-based hypertext system capable of storing and providing access to the world's complete stock of textual material (the Docuverse). Nelson has taken considerable pains to ensure that the system is capable of uniquely referencing billions of items, their interrelationships and the copyright issues arising from their use and distribution. A key feature of Xanadu is the fact that a piece of text is only held once in the system irrespective of the number of documents in which it may occur.

Nelson, T.H. (1980) Replacing the printed word: a complete literary system. In S.H. Lavington (ed.) *Proceedings of the IFIP Congress.* Amsterdam: North-Holland. 1013–1023.

REFERENCES

Aaronson, D. and Ferres, S. (1986) Reading strategies for children and adults: a quantitative model. *Psychological Review*, 93(1), 89–112.

Alschuler, L. (1989) Hand-crafted hypertext: lessons from the ACM experiment. In E. Barrett (ed.) *The Society of Text: Hypertext, Hypermedia, and the Social Construction of Information*. Cambridge, MA: MIT Press.

Anderson, J. (1980) *Cognitive Psychology and its Implications*. San Francisco: W.H. Freeman.

Anderson, J.R. and Bower, G.H. (1973) *Human Associative Memory*. Washington, DC: Winston.

Angell, C. (1987) *Information, New Technology and Manpower: The Impact of New Technology on Demand for Information Specialists*. LIR Report 52. London: The British Library.

Baird, P. and Percival, M. (1989) Glasgow On-Line: database development using Apple's HyperCard. In R. McAleese (ed.) *Hypertext: Theory into Practice*. Oxford: Intellect.

Barnard, P., Morton, J., Long, J. and Ottley, P. (1977) Planning menus for display: some effects of their structure and content. IEE Conference Publication #150, 130–133.

Barrett, E. (1988) *Text, ConText, and HyperText*. Cambridge, MA: MIT Press.

Bartlett, F.C. (1932) *Remembering*. Cambridge: Cambridge University Press.

de Beaugrande, R. (1980) *Text, Discourse and Process*. Norwood, NJ: Ablex.

Beech, J. and Colley, A. (1987) *Cognitive Approaches to Reading*. Chichester: John Wiley.

Beeman, W.O., Anderson, K.T., Bader, G., Larkin, J., McClard, A.P., McQuilian, P. and Shields, M. (1987) Hypertext and pluralism: from lineal to non-lineal thinking. *Proceedings of Hypertext '87*. University of North Carolina, Chapel Hill. 67–88.

Benest, I.D. (1990) A hypertext system with controlled hype. In R. McAleese and C. Green (eds.) *Hypertext: State of the Art*. Oxford: Intellect.

Bereiter, C. and Scardamalia, M. (1987) *The Psychology of Written Composition*. Hillsdale, NJ: Lawrence Erlbaum Associates.

Billingsley, P. (1982) Navigation through hierarchical menu structures: does it help to have a map? *Proceedings of the Human Factors Society 26th Annual Meeting*.

Borich, G.D. and Jemelka, R.P. (1981) Evaluation. In H.F. O'Neil (ed.) *Computer-Based Instruction: A State-of-the-Art Assessment*. London: Academic Press.

Brown, P. (1987) Turning ideas into products: the Guide system. *Proceedings of Hypertext '87*, University of North Carolina, Chapel Hill. 33–40.

Brown, P. (1988) Hypertext — the way forward. In J.C. van Vliet (ed.) *Document Manipulation and Typography*. Cambridge: Cambridge University Press. 183–191.

Brown, P. (1989) Do we need maps to navigate around hypertext? *Electronic Publishing — origination, dissemination and design*, 2(2), 91–100.

Bunderson, C.V. (1974) The design and production of learner-controlled software for the TICCIT system: a progress report. *International Journal of Man-Machine Studies*, 6, 479–492.

Bush, V. (1945) As we may think. *Atlantic Monthly*, 176/1, July, 101–108.

Cakir, A., Hart, D.J. and Stewart, T.F.M. (1980) *Visual Display Terminals*. Chichester: John Wiley.

Campbell, R. and Stern, B. (1987) ADONIS — a new approach to document delivery. *Microcomputers for Information Management*, 4(2), 87–107.

Canter, D. (1984) Wayfinding and signposting: penance or prosthesis? In R. Easterby and H. Zuraga (eds.) *Information Design*. Chichester: John Wiley. 245–264.

Canter, D., Rivers, R. and Storrs, G. (1985) Characterising user navigation through complex data structures. *Behaviour and Information Technology*, 4(2), 93–102.

Carbonell, J.R. (1970) AI in CAI: an artificial-intelligence approach to computer assisted instruction. *IEEE Transactions on Man-Machine Systems*, MMS-11(4), 190–202.

Carroll, J. and Thomas, J. (1982) Metaphor and cognitive representation of computing systems. *IEEE Transactions on Systems Man and Cybernetics*, SMC-12(2), 107–116.

Chafe, W.L. (1982) Integration and involvement in speaking, writing and oral literature. In D. Tannen (ed.) *Spoken and Written Language: Exploring Orality and Literature*. Norwood, NJ: Ablex.

Charney, D. (1987) Comprehending non-linear text: the role of discourse cues and reading strategies. *Proceedings of Hypertext '87*, University of North Carolina, Chapel Hill. 109–120.

Chaytor, H.J. (1945) *From Script to Print*. London: Sidgwick and Jackson.

Clanchy, M.T. (1979) *From Memory to Written Record*. London: Edward Arnold.

Clark, H. (1977) Inferences in comprehension. In D. Laberge and S. Samuels (eds.) *Basic Processes in Reading: Perception and Comprehension*. Norwood, NJ: Ablex.

Clarke, A. (1981) The use of serials at the British Library Lending Division. *Interlending Review*, 9, 111–117.

Collier, G.H. (1987) Thoth-II: hypertext with explicit semantics. *Proceedings of Hypertext '87*, University of North Carolina, Chapel Hill. 269–289.

Collins, A.M. and Loftus, E.F. (1975) A spreading activation theory of semantic processing. *Psychological Review*, 82, 407–428.

Collins, A.M. and Quillian, M.R. (1969) Retrieval time from semantic memory. *Journal of Verbal Learning and Verbal Behavior*, 8, 240–247.

Coltheart, V. and Evans, J. (1982) An investigation of semantic memory in individuals. *Memory and Cognition*, 9(5), 524–532.

Conklin, J. (1987) Hypertext: an introduction and survey. *Computer*, September, 17–41.

Cooke, P. and Williams, I. (1989) Design issues in large hypertext systems for technical documentation. In R. McAleese (ed.) *Hypertext: Theory into Practice*. Oxford: Intellect.

Creed, A., Dennis, I. and Newstead, S. (1987) Proof-reading on VDUs. *Behaviour and Information Technology*, 6(1), 3–13.

Crowder, R. (1982) *The Psychology of Reading: An Introduction*. Oxford: Oxford University Press.

Dantzig, T. (1954) *Number: The Language of Science*. London: George Allen & Unwin.

Diaper, D. and Rada, R. (1989) Expertext: hyperising expert systems and expertising hypertext. In *Proceedings of the Conference on Hypermedia/Hypertext and Object Oriented Databases*. Uxbridge: Unicom.

van Dijk, T.A., (1980) *Macrostructures*. Hillsdale, NJ: Lawrence Erlbaum Associates.

van Dijk, T.A. and Kintsch, W. (1983) *Strategies of Discourse Comprehension*. New York: Academic Press.

Dillon, A. (1990a) Readers' models of text structures: some experimental findings. HUSAT Memo Nº 516, HUSAT Research Institute, Loughborough University.

Dillon, A. (1990b) A framework for the design of usable electronic text. Unpublished PhD thesis, Loughborough University.

Dillon, A. and McKnight, C. (1990) Towards a classification of text types: a repertory grid approach. *International Journal of Man-Machine Studies*, 33, (in press).

Dillon, A., McKnight, C. and Richardson, J. (1988) Reading from paper versus reading from screens. *The Computer Journal*, 31(5), 457–464.

Dillon, A., Richardson, J. and McKnight, C. (1989) The human factors of journal usage and the design of electronic text, *Interacting with Computers*, 1(2), 183–189.

Downs, R. and Stea, D. (1977) *Maps in Minds: Reflections on Cognitive Mapping*, New York: Harper and Row.

Downs, R. and Stea, D. (1973)(eds.) *Image and Environment: Cognitive Mapping and Spatial Behaviour*. London: Edward Arnold.

Duchastel, P. (1988) Display and interaction features of instructional texts and computers. *British Journal of Educational Technology*, 19(1), 58–65.

Duffy, T.M. and Knuth, R.A. (1990) Hypermedia and instruction: where is the match? In D.H. Jonassen and H. Mandl (eds.) *Designing Hypermedia for Learning*. Heidelberg: Springer-Verlag.

Dugdale, S. (1982) Green Globs: a microcomputer application for graphing of equations. *Mathematics Teacher*, 75, 208–214.

Duncan, E.B. (1989) A faceted approach to hypertext. In R. McAleese (ed.) *Hypertext: Theory into Practice*. Oxford: Intellect.

Edwards, D. and Hardman, L. (1989) "Lost in hyperspace": cognitive mapping and navigation in a hypertext environment. In R. McAleese (ed.) *Hypertext:Theory into Practice*. Oxford: Intellect.

Egan, D., Remde, J., Landauer, T., Lochbaum, C. and Gomez, L. (1989) Behavioral evaluation and analysis of a hypertext browser. In *Proceedings of CHI'89*. New York: Association of Computing Machinery. 205–210.

Eisenstein, E. (1979) *The Printing Press as an Agent of Change*. Cambridge: Cambridge University Press.

Elm, W. and Woods, D. (1985) Getting lost: a case study in interface design. *Proceedings of the Human Factors Society 29th Annual Meeting*, 927–931.

Engst, A.C. (1989) *Descent into the Maelstrom*. Hyperfiction available from the author, RD #1 Box 53, Richford, NY 13835.

Evans, M. (1980) The geometry of the mind. *Architecture Association Quarterly*, 12, 32–55.

Garnham, A. (1986) *Mental Models as Representations of Text and Discourse*. Chichester: Ellis Horwood.

Glushko, R.J. (1989) Transforming text into hypertext for a compact disc encyclopedia. *Proceedings of CHI'89*. New York: Association of Computing Machinery.

Goody, J. (1977) *The Domestication of the Savage Mind*. Cambridge: Cambridge University Press.

Gordon, S., Gustavel, J., Moore, J. and Hankey, J. (1988) The effects of hypertext on reader knowledge representation. *Proceedings of the Human Factors Society 32nd Annual Meeting*, 296–300.

Gould, J.D. and Grischkowsky, N. (1984) Doing the same work with hard copy and cathode-ray tube (CRT) computer terminals. *Human Factors,* 26(3), 323–337.

Gould, J.D., Alfaro, L., Finn, R., Haupt, B. and Minuto, A. (1987) Reading from CRT displays can be as fast as reading from paper. *Human Factors*, 26(5), 497–517.

Hagelbarger, D. and Thompson, R. (1983) Experiments in teleterminal design. *IEEE Spectrum*, 20, 40–45.

Halasz, F.G. (1987) Reflections on NoteCards: seven issues for the next generation of hypermedia systems. *Proceedings of Hypertext '87*. University of North Carolina, Chapel Hill. 345–365.

Halasz, F.G., Moran, T.P. and Trigg, R.H. (1987) NoteCards in a nutshell. *Proceedings of the ACM CHI+GI Conference*, Toronto. 45–52.

Hammond, N. (1989) Hypermedia and learning: who guides whom? In H. Maurer (ed.) *Computer Assisted Learning*. Berlin: Springer-Verlag.

Hammond, N. and Allinson, L. (1987) The travel metaphor as design principle and training aid for navigating around complex systems. In D. Diaper and R. Winder (eds.) *People and Computers III*. Cambridge: Cambridge University Press.

Hammond, N. and Allinson, L. (1989) Extending hypertext for learning: an investigation of access and guidance tools. In A. Sutcliffe and L. Macaulay (eds.) *People and Computers V*. Cambridge: Cambridge University Press.

Hartley, J. (1978) *Designing Instructional Text*. London: Kogan Page.

Havelock, E. A. (1980) The coming of literate communication to Western culture. *Journal of Communication*, 30, 90–98.

Havelock, E.A. (1963) *Preface to Plato*. Oxford: Blackwell.

Havelock, E.A. (1976) *The Origins of Western Literacy*. Monograph Series 14. Toronto: The Ontario Institute for Studies in Education.

Holloway, H.L. (1987) *An Introduction to Generic Coding and SGML*. British Library Research Paper 27. London: The British Library.

Howell, G. (1990) Hypertext meets interactive fiction: new vistas in creative writing. In R. McAleese and C. Green (eds.) *Hypertext: State of the Art*. Oxford: Intellect.

Huey, E.B. (1908) *The Psychology and Pedagogy of Reading*. New York: Macmillan.

James, W. (1950) *The Principles of Psychology*. New York: Dover.

Johnson-Laird, P. (1983) *Mental Models*. Cambridge: Cambridge University Press.

Jonassen, D.H. (1982) *The Technology of Text*. Englewood Cliffs, NJ: Educational Technology Publications.

Jonassen, D.H. (1986) Hypertext principles for text and courseware design. *Educational Psychologist*, 21(4), 269–292.

Jonassen, D.H. (1990) Semantic network elicitation: tools for structuring hypertext. In R. McAleese and C. Green (eds.) *Hypertext: State of the Art*. Oxford: Intellect.

Jonassen, D.H. and Mandl, H. (1990)(eds.) *Designing Hypermedia for Learning*. Heidelberg: Springer-Verlag.

Jones, T. (1989) Incidental learning during information retrieval: a hypertext experiment. In H. Maurer (ed.) *Computer Assisted Learning*. Berlin: Springer-Verlag.

Jones, W.P. and Dumais, S.T. (1986) The spatial metaphor for user interfaces: experimental tests of reference by location versus name. *Association of Computing Machinery Transactions on Office Information Systems*, 4(1), 42–63.

Just, M.A. and Carpenter, P. (1980) A theory of reading: from eye movements to comprehension. *Psychological Review*, 87(4), 329–354.

Kak, A.V. (1981) Relationships between readability of printed and CRT-displayed text. *Proceedings of Human Factors Society 25th Annual Meeting*, 137–140.

Kelly, G.A. (1955) *The Psychology of Personal Constructs*. New York: Norton.

Kelly, V. (1984) Microcomputers and the curriculum — uses and abuses. In V. Kelly (ed.) *Microcomputers and the Curriculum*. London: Harper & Row.

Kibby, M.R. and Mayes, J.T. (1989) Towards intelligent hypertext. In R. McAleese (ed.) *Hypertext: Theory into Practice*. Oxford: Intellect.

Kieras, D.E. (1985) Thematic processes in the comprehension of technical prose. In B.K. Britton and J.B. Black (eds.) *Understanding Expository Prose*. Hillsdale, NJ: Lawrence Erlbaum Associates.

Kintsch, W. (1974) *The Representation of Meaning in Memory*. Hillsdale, NJ: Lawrence Erlbaum Associates.

Kintsch, W. and van Dijk, T.A. (1978) Towards a model of text comprehension and production. *Psychological Review*, 85, 363–394.

Kintsch,W. and Yarborough, J. (1982) The role of rhetorical structure in text comprehension. *Journal of Educational Psychology*, 74, 828–834.

Kruskal, J.B. (1964) Multidimensional scaling by optimizing goodness of fit to a non-metric hypothesis. *Psychometrica*, 29, 1–27.

Kutz, R.E. (1985) The computer as a learning tool. In S. Harlow (ed.) *Humanistic Perspectives on Computers in the Schools*. New York: Haworth Press.

Landow, G. (1990) The rhetoric of hypermedia: a guide for authors. In D. Jonassen and H. Mandl (eds.) *Designing Hypermedia for Learning*. Heidelberg: Springer-Verlag.

Lee, E., Whalen, T., McEwen, S.and Latrémouille, S. (1984) Optimising the design of menu pages for information retrieval. *Ergonomics*, 27(10), 1051–1069.

Leggett, J.L., Schnase, J.L. and Kacmar, C.J. (1990) Hypertext for learning. In D.H. Jonassen and H. Mandl (eds.) *Designing Hypermedia for Learning*. Heidelberg: Springer-Verlag.

Lord, A. (1960) *The Singer of Tales*. Harvard Studies in Comparative Literature 24. Cambridge, MA: Harvard University Press.

Lovelace, E.A. and Southall, S.D. (1983) Memory for words in prose and their locations on the page. *Memory and Cognition*, 11(5), 429–434.

Luria, A.R. (1976) *Cognitive Development: Its Cultural and Social Foundations*. Cambridge, MA: Harvard University Press.

Marchionini, G. (1990) Evaluating hypermedia-based learning. In D.H. Jonassen and H. Mandl (eds.) *Designing Hypermedia for Learning*. Heidelberg: Springer-Verlag.

Marchionini, G. and Shneiderman, B. (1988) Finding facts versus browsing knowledge in hypertext systems. *Computer*, January, 70–80.

McAleese, R. (1989a) Navigation and browsing in hypertext. In R. McAleese (ed.) *Hypertext:Theory into Practice*. Oxford: Intellect.

McAleese, R. (1989b)(ed.) *Hypertext: Theory into Practice*. Oxford: Intellect.

McClelland, J. and Rumelhart D. (1981) An interactive activation model of context effects in letter perception. Part I: An account of basic findings. *Psychological Review*, 88, 375–407.

McConkie, G. and Rayner, K. (1975) The span of the effective stimulus during a fixation in reading. *Perception and Psychophysics*, 17, 578–586.

McKnight, C., Dillon, A. and Richardson, J. (1990) A comparison of linear and hypertext formats in information retrieval. In R. McAleese and C. Green (eds.) *Hypertext: State of the Art*. Oxford: Intellect.

McKnight, C., Richardson, J. and Dillon, A. (1990) Journal articles as learning resource: what can hypertext offer? In D.H. Jonassen and H. Mandl (eds.) *Designing Hypermedia for Learning*. Heidelberg: Springer-Verlag.

McLuhan, M. (1962) *The Gutenberg Galaxy*. Toronto: University of Toronto Press.

McLuhan, M. (1964) *Understanding Media*. London: Routledge and Kegan Paul.

Megarry, J. (1988) Hypertext and compact discs — the challenge of multi-media learning. *British Journal of Educational Technology*, 19, 172–183.

Mendoza, S. and Thomas, L.F. (1972) The individual's construction of his visual world as projected by the repertory grid. Paper presented to the Annual Conference of the British Psychological Society, April, University of Nottingham.

Meyer, B.J.F. (1975) *The Organization of Prose and its Effect on Memory*. Amsterdam: North-Holland.

Miller, G.A. (1956) The magical number seven, plus or minus two: some limits on our capacity for processing information. *Psychological Review*, 63, 81–97.

Monk, A., Walsh, P. and Dix, A. (1988) A comparison of hypertext, scrolling, and folding as mechanisms for program browsing. In D. Jones and R. Winder (eds.) *People and Computers IV*. Cambridge: Cambridge University Press.

Muter, P., Latrémouille, S.A., Treurniet, W.C. and Beam, P. (1982) Extended reading of continuous text on television screens. *Human Factors*, 24(5), 501–508.

Nelson, T.H. (1981) *Literary Machines*. Paper version available from the author, 8480 Fredericksburg #138, San Antonio, TX 78229; also to be published in the UK by Intellect. Electronic version available from Office Workstations Ltd, Rosebank House, 144 Broughton Road, Edinburgh EH7 4LE.

Nelson, T.H. (1988) Managing immense storage. *Byte*, January, 225–238.

Nelson, T.H. (1989) Keynote Address given to the Hypertext II conference, University of York, June.

Niblett, T. and van Hoff, A. (1989) Structured hypertext documents via SGML. Poster presentation at Hypertext II, University of York, June.

Nisbett, R. and Wilson, T. (1977) Telling more than we can know: verbal reports on mental processes. *Psychological Review,* 84, 231–259.

Norman, D.A. (1976) Studies in learning and self-contained educational systems, 1973–1976. Technical Report Nº 7601. Washington, DC: Office of Naval Research, Advanced Research Projects Agency.

Norman, D.A. (1986) Cognitive engineering. In D.A. Norman and S.W. Draper (eds.) *User Centred System Design.* Hillsdale, NJ: Lawrence Erlbaum Associates.

Norman, D.A., Gentner, D.R. and Stevens, A.L. (1976) Comments on learning schemata and memory representation. In D. Klahr (ed.) *Cognition and Instruction.* Hillsdale, NJ: Lawrence Erlbaum Associates.

O'Neil, H.F. and Paris, J. (1981) Introduction and overview of computer-based instruction. In H.F. O'Neil (ed.) *Computer-Based Instruction: A State-of-the-Art Assessment.* London: Academic Press.

O'Shea, T. and Self, J. (1983) *Learning and Teaching with Computers.* Brighton: Harvester Press.

Olsen, J. (1989) Contribution to symposium on 'Tasks, texts and functionality' at the Hypertext II conference, University of York, June.

Olshavsky, J. (1977) Reading as problem solving: an investigation of strategies. *Reading Research Quarterly*, 4, 654–674.

Olson, D.R. (1977) From utterance to text: The bias of language in speech and writing. *Harvard Educational Review*, 47(3), 257–281.

Ong, W.J. (1971) *Rhetoric, Romance and Technology: Studies in the Interaction of Expression and Culture.* Ithaca: Cornell University Press

Ong, W.J. (1982) *Orality and Literacy: The Technologizing of the Word.* London: Methuen.

Osgood, C.E., Suci, G.J. and Tannenbaum, P.H. (1957) *The Measurement of Meaning.* University of Illinois Press.

Papert, S. (1980) *Mindstorms: Children, Computers and Powerful Ideas.* Brighton: Harvester Press.

Parry, M. (1971) *The Making of Homeric Verse: The Collected Papers of Milman Parry.* Oxford: Clarendon Press.

Pugh, A. (1979) Styles and strategies in adult silent reading. In P. Kolers, M. Wrolstad and H. Bouma (eds.) *Processing of Visible Language 1.* London: Plenum Press.

Rada, R. and Barlow, J. (1989) Expert systems and hypertext. *Knowledge Engineering Review*, 3, 285 – 301.

Rada, R., Keith, B., Burgoine, M. and Reid, D. (1989) Collaborative writing of text and hypertext. *Hypermedia*, 1(2), 93–110.

Rahtz, S., Carr, L. and Hall, W. (1990) Creating multimedia documents: hypertext processing. In R. McAleese and C. Green (eds.) *Hypertext: State of the Art.* Oxford: Intellect.

Richardson, J., Dillon, A. and McKnight, C. (1989) The effect of window size on reading and manipulating electronic text. In E.D. Megaw (ed.) *Contemporary Ergonomics 1989*. London: Taylor and Francis.

Richardson, J., McKnight, C., Dillon, A. and Forrester, M. (1989) An experimental investigation of the manipulation and comprehension of screen-presented text. HUSAT Memo № 432, HUSAT Research Institute, Loughborough University.

Rothkopf, E.Z. (1971) Incidental memory for location of information in text. *Journal of Verbal Learning and Verbal Behavior*, 10, 608–613.

Rumelhart, D.E. and Ortony, A. (1977) The representation of knowledge in memory. In R.C. Anderson, R.J. Shapiro and W.E. Montague (eds.) *Schooling and the Acquisition of Knowledge*. Hillsdale, NJ: Lawrence Erlbaum Associates.

Rumelhart, D.E., Lindsay, P.H. and Norman, D.A. (1972) A process model for long term memory. In E. Tulving and W. Donaldson (eds.) *Organization of Memory*. New York: Academic Press.

Saenger, P. (1982) Silent reading. *Viator*, 13, 367–414.

Schank, R. and Abelson, R. (1977) *Scripts, Plans, Goals, and Understanding*. Hillsdale, NJ: Lawrence Erlbaum Associates.

Schumacher, G. and Waller, R. (1985) Testing design alternatives: a comparison of procedures. In T. Duffy and R. Waller (eds.) *Designing Usable Texts*. Orlando, FL: Academic Press.

Scribner, S. and Cole, M. (1981) *The Psychology of Literacy*. Cambridge, MA: Harvard University Press.

Shneiderman, B. (1987a) *Designing the User Interface: Strategies for Effective Human-Computer Interaction*. Reading, MA: Addison-Wesley

Shneiderman, B. (1987b) User interface design and evaluation for an electronic encyclopedia. In G. Salvendy (ed.) *Cognitive Engineering in the Design of Human-Computer Interaction and Expert Systems*. Amsterdam: Elsevier. 207–223.

Simpson, A. (1989) Navigation in hypertext: design issues. Paper presented at International OnLine 89 Conference, London, December.

Simpson, A. and McKnight, C. (1990) Navigation in hypertext: structural cues and mental maps. In R. McAleese and C. Green (eds.) *Hypertext: State of the Art*. Oxford: Intellect.

Skinner, B.F. (1968) *The Technology of Teaching*. New York: Appleton-Century-Crofts.

Smith, C.S. (1981) Structural hierarchy in science, art and history. In *A Search for Structure — Selected Essays on Science, Art and History*. Cambridge, MA: MIT Press.

Smith, J.B., Weiss, S.F. and Ferguson, G.J. (1987) A hypertext writing environment and its cognitive basis. *Proceedings of Hypertext '87*, University of North Carolina, Chapel Hill. 195–214.

Snowberry, K., Parkinson , S. and Sisson, N. (1985) Effects of help fields on navigating through hierarchical menu structures. *International Journal of Man-Machine Studies*, 22, 479–491.

Stanton, N.A. and Stammers, R.B. (1989) A comparison of structured and unstructured navigation through a computer based training package for a simulated industrial task. Paper presented to the Symposium on Computer Assisted Learning — CAL 89, University of Surrey.

Stanton, N.A. and Stammers, R.B. (1990) Learning styles in a non-linear training environment. In R. McAleese and C. Green (eds.) *Hypertext: State of the Art*. Oxford: Intellect.

Streitz, N.A. (1990) A cognitive approach for the design of authoring tools in hypertext environments. In D.H. Jonassen and H. Mandl (eds.) *Designing Hypermedia for Learning*. Heidelberg: Springer-Verlag.

Tannen, D. (1982) The oral/literate continuum in discourse. In D. Tannen (ed.) *Spoken and Written Language: Exploring Orality and Literature*. Norwood, NJ: Ablex.

Thorndyke, P. (1977) Cognitive structures in comprehension and memory of narrative discourse, *Cognitive Psychology*, 9, 77–110.

Thorndyke, P. and Hayes-Roth, B. (1982) Differences in spatial knowledge acquired from maps and navigation. *Cognitive Psychology*, 14, 560–589.

Tolman, E.C. (1948) Cognitive maps in rats and men, *Psychological Review*, 55, 189–208.

Tombaugh, J. and McEwen, S. (1982) Comparison of two information retrieval methods on Videotex: tree structure versus alphabetical directory. *Proceedings of the Conference on Human Factors in Computer Systems*. Gaithersburg, MD: Association of Computing Machinery. 106–110.

Trigg, R.H. (1983) A network-based approach to text handling for the online scientific community. PhD thesis, University of Maryland.

Trigg, R.H. and Irish, P.M. (1987) Hypertext habitats: experiences of writers in NoteCards. *Proceedings of Hypertext '87*, University of North Carolina, Chapel Hill. 89–108.

Trigg, R.H. and Suchman, L.A. (1989) Collaborative writing in NoteCards. In R. McAleese (ed.) *Hypertext: Theory into Practice*. Oxford: Intellect.

Verreck, W.A. and Lkoundi, A. (1990) From instructional text to instructional hypertext: an experiment. In D.H. Jonassen and H. Mandl (eds.) *Designing Hypermedia for Learning*. Heidelberg: Springer-Verlag.

Waller, R (1987) The typographic contribution to language: towards a model of typographic genres and their underlying structures. Unpublished PhD Thesis, University of Reading.

Wells, H.G. (1938) World Encyclopaedia. In *World Brain*. New York: Doubleday, Doran. Originally presented at the Royal Institution of Great Britain weekly evening meeting, Friday November 20, 1936.

Wetherell, A. (1979) Short-term memory for verbal and graphic route information. *Proceedings of the Human Factors Society 23rd Annual Meeting*.

Whalley, P. (1990) Models of hypertext structure and learning. In D.H. Jonassen and H. Mandl (eds.) *Designing Hypermedia for Learning*. Heidelberg: Springer-Verlag.

Whalley, P. and Fleming, R. (1975) An experiment with a simple recorder of reading behaviour. *Programmed Learning and Educational Technology*, 12, 120–124.

Wickens, C. (1984) *Engineering Psychology and Human Performance.* Columbus, OH: Charles Merrill.

Wilkinson, R.T. and Robinshaw, H.M. (1987) Proof-reading: VDU and paper text compared for speed, accuracy and fatigue. *Behaviour and Information Technology*, 6(2), 125–133.

Witty, F.J. (1965) Early indexing techniques: a study of several book indexes of the 14th, 15th and early 16th centuries. *The Library Quarterly*, 35(3), 141–148.

Wright, P. (1980) Textual literacy: an outline sketch of psychological research on reading and writing. In P. Kolers, M. Wrolstad and H. Bouma (eds.) *Processing of Visible Language 2.* London: Plenum Press.

Wright, P. (1987) Reading and writing for electronic journals. In B. Britton and S. Glynn (eds.) *Executive Control Processes in Reading.* Hillsdale, NJ: Lawrence Erlbaum Associates.

Wright, P. and Lickorish, A. (1983) Proof-reading texts on screen and paper. *Behaviour and Information Technology*, 2(3), 227–235.

Wright, P. and Lickorish, A. (1989) The influence of discourse structure on display and navigation in hypertexts. In N. Williams and P. Holt (eds.) *Computers and Writing.* Oxford: Intellect. 90–124.

Wright, P. and Lickorish, A. (1990) An empirical comparison of two navigation systems for two hypertexts. In R. McAleese and C. Green (eds.) *Hypertext: State of the Art.* Oxford: Intellect.

Yeates, F. (1966) *The Art of Memory.* London: Routledge and Kegan Paul.

Zechmeister, E. and McKillip, J. (1972) Recall of place on a page. *Journal of Educational Psychology*, 63, 446–453.

Zechmeister, E., McKillip, J., Pasko, S. and Bespalec, D. (1975) Visual memory for place on the page. *Journal of General Psychology*, 92, 43–52.

AUTHOR INDEX

SUBJECT INDEX